Libra

MATHS & ENGLISH FOR
BUSINESS
ADMINISTRATION

Graduated exercises and practice exam

Andrew Spencer and Carole Vella

CENGAGE
Learning·

145859

Australia · Brazil · Japan · Korea · Mexico · Singapore · Spain · United Kingdom · United States

Maths & English for Business Administration

Andrew Spencer and Carole Vella

Publishing Director: Linden Harris

Publisher: Lucy Mills

Development Editor: Claire Napoli

Editorial Assistant: Lauren Darby

Production Editor: Alison Burt

Manufacturing Buyer: Eyvett Davis

Typesetter: Cambridge Publishing Management Limited

Cover design: HCT Creative

For product information and technology assistance, contact **emea.info@cengage.com**.

For permission to use material from this text or product, and for permission queries, email **emea.permissions@cengage.com**.

This work is adapted from *Pre Apprenticeship: Maths & Literacy Series* by Andrew Spencer published by Cengage Learning Australia Pty Limited © 2010.

British Library Cataloguing-in-Publication Data
A catalogue record for this book is available from the British Library.

ISBN: 978-1-4080-8309-3

Cengage Learning EMEA Cheriton House, North Way, Andover, Hampshire, SP10 5BE United Kingdom

Cengage Learning products are represented in Canada by Nelson Education Ltd.

For your lifelong learning solutions, visit **www.cengage.co.uk**

Purchase your next print book, e-book or e-chapter at **www.cengagebrain.com**

Printed in Greece by Bakis
1 2 3 4 5 6 7 8 9 10 – 15 14 13

Maths & English for Business Administration

Contents

Introduction

Functional skills are essential skills in English and mathematics that enable everyone to deal with the practical problems and challenges of life – at home, in education and at work. They are essential to all our lives. For example, they help us recognize good value deals when making purchases, in writing an effective application letter, or when using the internet to access local services or online banking. They are about using English, mathematics and ICT in everyday situations.

Functional skills are a key to success. They open doors to learning, to life and to work. These skills are valued by employers and further education institutions and are a platform on which to build other employability skills. Better functional skills can mean a better future – as learners or as employees.

Functional skills are an essential part of the secondary curriculum. They are embedded in the revised Programmes of Study for English, mathematics and ICT at Key Stage 3 and Key Stage 4, and in the revised GCSE subject criteria for these subjects. They are a mandatory component of Diplomas, the Foundation Learning Tier (FLT) and Apprenticeships. They will also be available as stand-alone qualifications for young people and adults. Functional skills are based on a problem-solving approach and should be developed in a practical way through discussion, thinking and explanation, across the whole 11–19 curriculum.

It is therefore important to recognize and promote awareness that functional skills are essential for:

- getting the most from education and training
- the personal development of all young people and adults
- independence – enabling learners to manage in a variety of situations
- developing employability skills
- giving people a sound basis for further learning.

The implications for teaching and learning are significant and will need to be introduced gradually and thoughtfully, but they do not threaten aspects of existing good practice. Helping learners to become more 'functional' is supported by existing practices including:

- a focus on applied learning
- learner-centred approaches
- active learning and a problem-centred approach
- partnership learning
- assessment for learning.

The skills in this book are tailored to a student working in Business Administration by developing their employability skills. Commonly used industry terms are introduced so that students have a basic understanding of terminology that they will encounter in the workplace environment (words that are in the glossary appear in **bold** the first time they are used). Students who can complete this workbook and reach a higher outcome in all topics will have achieved the goal of this resource.

About the authors

Andrew Spencer has studied education both within Australia and overseas. He has a Bachelor of Education, as well as a Masters of Science in which he specialized in teacher education. Andrew has extensive experience in teaching secondary mathematics throughout New South Wales and South Australia for well over fifteen years. He has taught a range of subject areas including Maths, English, Science, Classics, Physical Education and Technical Studies. His sense of the importance of practical mathematics continued to develop with the range of subject areas he taught in.

Carole Vella studied Business Studies in the UK. She has a Bachelor of Arts in Business Management and Information Technology, as well as a Masters of Business Administration. Carole has extensive experience in teaching and examining Business Studies in the UK for over 12 years. She has taught a range of subject areas, including Business Administration, Retail, Marketing, Human Resources and Economics.

Acknowledgements

Andrew Spencer:
>   For Paula, Zach, Katelyn, Mum and Dad.
>   Many thanks to Mal Aubrey (GTA) and all training organizations for their input.
>   To the De La Salle Brothers for their selfless work with all students.
>   Thanks also to Dr Pauline Carter for her unwavering support for all maths teachers.
>   This is for all students who value learning, who are willing to work hard and who have character …
>   and are characters!

Carole Vella:
>   For Richard and Mum.

The publisher would like to thank the many copyright holders who have kindly granted us permission to reproduce material throughout this text. Every effort has been made to contact all rights holders, but in the unlikely event that anything has been overlooked, please contact the publisher directly and we will happily make the necessary arrangements at the earliest opportunity.

ENGLISH

Unit 1: Speaking, Listening and Communication

Short-answer questions

Specific instructions to students

- These are exercises to help you to make relevant and extended contributions to discussions, allowing for and responding to others' input.
- They will also help you prepare for and contribute to the formal discussion of ideas and opinions.
- They will help you to make different kinds of contributions to discussions and present information/points of view clearly and in appropriate language.
- Read the activities below, then answer accordingly.

Task 1: Conversation skills

Using a timer, hold a conversation with a partner for five minutes about health and safety in the office. After the five minutes, write below how you feel that conversation went (Was it successful? What were the good points? What were the bad points?).

Answer:

Task 2: Speaking and Listening

Using this list of scenarios, with a partner or small group, perform the role-play giving and receiving instructions, explanations and descriptions.

a   A customer asks for directions to your office, as they have a meeting there tomorrow.

What skills have you learnt?

_____

Give an example of another situation when you would use these communication skills.

_____

b   Your company is looking for ways of improving its service to customers so all staff are invited to a meeting to brainstorm ideas.

What skills have you learnt?

_____

Give an example of another situation in which you would use these communication skills.

_____

c   Your photocopier in the office has been broken now for two days and there is still no sign of the engineer. You ring them to complain.

What skills have you learnt?

_____

Give an example of another situation in which you would use these communication skills.

_____

Unit 2: Spelling and Proofreading Skills

Short-answer questions

Specific instructions to students

- This is an exercise to help you to identify and correct spelling errors.
- Read the activity below, then answer accordingly.

Task 1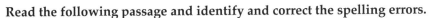

Read the following passage and identify and correct the spelling errors.

The receptionst arives at the office at 8.45 a.m. She checks the apointments book and notices that there are three customers to see one of the managers between 9.00 a.m. and 9.30 a.m. She then begins preparing for a busy Friday, as this is usually the day of the week that the payroll and banking are done. Her first job is to begin to look over the acounts payeble and acounts recievable. Several accounts need to be paid so the receptionist begins on them immediately. The payroll needed to be double-checked, to make sure all payment records are acurate. This ensured that all employes would get paid on time and everyone would receve their pay. Once this was completed, the receptionist started on the banking. The petty cash box was checked for invoices and any other cover notes that show that money had been taken from the box. All the money balanced out and the banking of the petty cash could be done later that day.

The recetionist began preparing lunch for the managor and the customers that he had been in a conferance with during the morning. Special care was taken with the food preperation as in the previous week several staff had come down with food poisoning and the managemant had sent out a memo asking all staff to be diligent about washing their hands before preparing food.

Incorrect words:

Correct words:

Task 2 (L2)

Some of the words in the text are in **bold and blue**

Look up these words in a dictionary, and write the meaning below:

Answer:

checks

_____

immediately

_____

invoices

_____

diligent

_____

Task 3: Different types of text (L2)

There are four different types of text:

- Instructive
  Instructive texts tell you what to do.

- Persuasive
  Persuasive texts try to convince you to do something.

- Informative
  Informative texts give you information about something.

- Descriptive
  Descriptive texts describe things to you in detail.

QUESTION 1

What type of text are the following terms?

a   Comfortable

Answer:

_____

b   Good-sized

Answer:

_____

c   Needs minor renovations

Answer:

_____

QUESTION 2

Write a short piece to persuade someone to buy the house in the picture.

Answer:

Short-answer questions

Specific instructions to students

- The following questions will help you practise your grammar and punctuation.
- Read the following questions, then answer accordingly.

QUESTION 1

Which linking word or phrase could you use instead of 'whereas'?

Answer:

_____

QUESTION 2

What does the linking word 'alternatively' mean?

Answer:

_____

QUESTION 3

What punctuation is missing from the following sentence?

> A receptionist is trained to type memos letters e-mails reports answer the telephone and record the minutes of a meeting.

Answer:

_____

QUESTION 4

What is wrong with the following text? Correct the following sentences.

> Last Saturday the office was extremely busy; Lorraine was run off her feet with all the meetings that had been scheduled. She was pleased that she had remembered to ask fiona to come in to help. She had felt a bit guilty as she had had to ask fiona to travel in from manchester, where she had been on a hen night the night before.

Answer:

_____

_____

QUESTION 5

What is wrong with the following text?

> Why not apply for a Business Admin Apprenticeship at Balham College? Youll be able to gain excellent IT skills. To find out more, call Balham College reception on 01435 778367.

Answer:

_____

_____

QUESTION 6

Can you identify the mistake in this job application letter?

> Dear Madam
>
> I wish to apply for the vacancy of administration assistant at your Gloucester branch, as advertised in this week's Gloucester Globe.
>
> I have just completed my Level 2 NVQ Diploma in Business Administration coarse at Dinsdale Park College and am now looking for work in the Gloucester area.
>
> I enclose a copy of my CV and look forward to hearing from you.
>
> Yours faithfully
>
> Matthew Morris

Answer:

_____

QUESTION 7

a Add the missing full stops, commas and capital letters to this text telling you about an administrator handling mail.

Handling Mail

it is important for those working in administrative roles to have a good understanding of how to handle mail to ensure the flow of communication meets an organization's administrative needs it is equally important that they recognize the benefits of efficient mail distribution and of the negative impact of inaccuracies or delays an administrator should be able to sort and distribute incoming mail collecting sorting and despatching outgoing mail and considering how to deal with damaged or suspicious items

Answer:

QUESTION 8

Add commas to the following text to make the sense clearer.

Why it is important to an organization that visitors are made welcome?

Visitors who could be suppliers or customers will receive a positive impression of the organization and this may lead to e.g. a positive appointment or meeting increased business in future due to them telling other organizations how welcoming you are.

Answer:

QUESTION 9

Use a conjunction to complete each sentence. (Conjunctions are linking words that we can use to join up two sentences, for example: and, if, because, although, as, or, so.)

a   My name is David _____ I am an office worker.

b   I live in Wolverhampton now _____ I was born in Wales.

c   I am on reception today _____ my colleague Carole is off sick.

d   I want to pass my functional level 1 English _____ I must work hard in class.

e   I am very tired today _____ it was the staff party last night.

QUESTION 10

Write five sentences relating to what you do at work and ensure that you use different conjunctions to the sentences in Question 9.

a

_____

_____

b

_____

_____

c

_____

_____

d

_____

_____

e

_____

_____

Short-answer questions

Specific instructions to students

- This is an exercise to help you understand what you read.
- Read the following activity, then answer the questions that follow.

Comprehension Task 1

Read the following passage and answer the questions in sentence form.

It was 11.45 a.m., and nearly lunch time. Susan, who was the junior administrator, was looking forward to her lunch break. Within a few minutes Sarah, the Accounts Manager, entered the front office with a pile of documents in her hand. She spoke to Susan and said that a number of urgent tasks had come up. Sarah gave the papers to Susan and pointed out that there were several discrepancies in the balancing of the petty cash book. Unfortunately the credits and debits did not balance as Sarah had placed a number of receipts away in her drawer and had not forwarded them on to administration. Susan immediately began dividing up the documents into three separate piles: receipts for petty cash, invoices and delivery notes. Somehow the different documents had been mixed together and there was no order to them.

By two o'clock, Susan had everything under control. Fortunately, she had great administrative skills and she had also developed a unique ability to problem solve. When Sarah returned at 3.00 p.m. Susan explained that she had balanced the petty cash book and recorded all invoices on the computer's database. Susan had also filed copies of all documents and organized the delivery notes into the dates and times that parcels and orders had arrived and were sent. Both Sarah and Susan were pleased that they were able to catch up with the work but agreed to have a better system in place in the future. Susan suggested that all documents be placed in an 'in' tray as they arrived so that she could deal with all paperwork on a daily basis, which Sarah agreed was an excellent suggestion.

QUESTION 1

What was the problem with the petty cash book?

Answer:

QUESTION 2

What was the problem with the receipts and documents?

Answer:

_____

_____

QUESTION 3

How long did it take for Susan to get everything 'under control'?

Answer:

_____

QUESTION 4

How did Susan overcome the problems with the urgent tasks?

Answer:

_____

_____

_____

QUESTION 5

What was Susan's suggestion for the future so that the same problem was not repeated?

Answer:

_____

Comprehension Task 2

Read the following passage and answer the questions in sentence form.

> It was a busy Monday morning and Catherine the receptionist had arrived at work late due to a major accident on the M6 motorway. Suzannah, the Office Manager, was covering for her on reception as Catherine had telephoned to say she was running late.

As soon as she looked in her appointment book she noticed that the Warehouse Manager and Human Resource Manager were interviewing staff for the new vacancies in the refurbished warehouse and that the first candidate was due to arrive at 11.00 a.m.

Catherine needed to ensure that she had photocopied and organized all the relevant documentation including each candidate's application form and Curriculum Vitae, so that both the Warehouse Manager and Human Resources Manager had the correct documentation for the interview process.

Catherine showed all eight candidates to the interview room through the day and she telephoned the two candidates who didn't show to find out why they had not be able to make the interview that day.

She had truly had a busy day. Once the Warehouse Manager and Human Resource Manager had decided on the appropriate candidates for the warehousing positions, she began using her excellent IT skills processing the rejection letters to advise candidates that they had been unsuccessful.

QUESTION 1

Why was Catherine running late for work this morning?

Answer:

QUESTION 2

Why were interviews taking place today?

Answer:

QUESTION 3

What two documents did Catherine need to photocopy for the interview process?

Answer:

QUESTION 4

How many candidates should have been interviewed and how many turned up for the interview?

Answer:

QUESTION 5

What type of document was Catherine using her excellent IT skills to produce for each candidate who didn't get the job?

Answer:

Short-answer questions

Specific instructions to students

- The advert below was pinned on the office notice board. Look at the advert, and then answer the questions.

LEE PARK
FIREWORKS DISPLAY

Saturday 5th November
18.00 to 21.00

Fascinating fireworks and fantastic food

Every employee and family welcome.

**Limited tickets available.
Don't delay, book today!**

Lighting of the bonfire	18.30
Children's face painting and crafts	18.00–19.00
Food served	19.00–20.00
Fireworks	20.00–21.00

QUESTION 1

Where is the fireworks display taking place?

Answer:

_____

QUESTION 2

Name three things happening at this event.

Answer:

_____

_____

_____

QUESTION 3

This text is an advert. What are adverts designed to do? Tick the correct boxes.

(1) describe ☐   (2) inform ☐

(3) persuade ☐   (4) instruct ☐

QUESTION 4

Name three of the features used in this text.

Answer:

_____

_____

_____

QUESTION 5

The times in the text are in 24-hour format. Write the times again below in 12-hour format.

18.00 _____   18.30 _____

19.00 _____   20.00 _____

21.00 _____

QUESTION 6

What time will food be served?

Answer:

_____

QUESTION 7

The date on the text is written in the long form. Write the date again below in short form.

Answer:

_____

QUESTION 8

How long will the display last?

Answer:

_____

Unit 5: Homophones

Short-answer questions

Specific instructions to students

- The following questions relate to words that sound the same, but are spelt differently and have different meanings. These words are known as homophones.
- Read the questions carefully, then answer accordingly.

QUESTION 1

The following sentences are about two Business Administrators who have decided to go on holiday together.

a   Check your knowledge of *there, their* and *they're* in the following sentences. Only one sentence is correct. Which one is it?

   (1) They're are too many training courses booked whilst there away so they will have to be cancelled.

   (2) The manager realized that there holiday will be taken the same time as two others.

   (3) They're going on their holiday in the early hours of Friday morning.

   (4) There going to be short staffed all week so some staff may need to do overtime.

Answer:

_____

_____

b   Check your knowledge of *where, were* and *we're* in the following sentences. Only one sentence is correct. Which one is it?

   (1) When we get to our destination, we're not sure were we'll go first.

   (2) We're sure we'll be fine, when we know where we're going.

   (3) If there's a delay, where sure that we're going to miss our connecting flight.

   (4) Once we find the hotel, were going to shower and change and go straight out.

Answer:

_____

_____

c   Check your knowledge of *too, to* and *two* in the following sentences. Only one sentence is correct. Which one is it?

   (1) The two of us are going to go on holiday to New York too.

   (2) We want to go too Staten Island too.

   (3) We're concerned that there'll be two many people on the subway in New York.

   (4) To get too Staten Island, the two of us will need to catch the ferry.

Answer:

_____

_____

d   Check your knowledge of *buy, by* and *bye* in the following sentences. Only one sentence is correct. Which one is it?

   (1) We'll each have to bye a ticket to get to Staten Island by ferry.

   (2) By the way, we'll have to make sure that we buy plenty of souvenirs to take home.

   (3) Buy the time we get home, it will be a struggle to say bye to each other.

   (4) By all accounts, we'll have to bye some waterproofs for the ferry journey.

Answer:

_____

_____

e   Check your knowledge of *pause*, *paws* and *pours* in the following sentences. Only one sentence is correct. Which one is it?

   (1) If it paws down with rain, we'll go to Central Park Zoo.

   (2) If there's a pause in the rain, we'll go and see the polar bears.

   (3) It doesn't matter if their pours get wet, as they'll be swimming in their pool anyway.

   (4) Once it starts raining, though, it just paws and paws.

Answer:

_____

_____

f   Check your knowledge of *heal*, *he'll* and *heel* in the following sentences. Only one sentence is correct. Which one is it?

   (1) While running in the rain, I slipped and fell on my knee and broke the heal of my shoe.

   (2) My knee is really sore and bruised, so it will take a couple of days to heel.

   (3) I'm so glad that Andrew is with me, as he'll have to lend me a bit of support.

   (4) I couldn't find a cobbler, so I'll have to wait to get my heal fixed when I get home.

Answer:

_____

_____

QUESTION 2

Check your knowledge of *there*, *their* and *they're* in the following sentences. Read each sentence and write the correct word in the space provided, from the words provided below:

there   their   they're

a   The managers chose the shade of paint to complement the furniture in _____ office.

b   _____ was just enough seating in the reception area.

c   I wonder if I could fit another chair in reception, over _____?

d   I've asked the receptionist to welcome the customers and to hang up _____ coats for them.

e   It's nearly 11.00 a.m. and _____ going to be here in a minute.

f   There's a new range of coloured pens in stock; I've heard that _____ really good.

g   I believe that the office suppliers have got all of _____ new box files in stock.

h   I'll have to go to the office suppliers again. I was only _____ last week.

i   I must leave work on time to get to the office suppliers before _____ closed.

QUESTION 3

Check your knowledge of *where*, *were* and *we're* in the following sentences. Read each sentence and write the correct word in the space provided, from the words provided below:

where   were   we're

a   We always make sure that the interviewee is sitting _____ they feel comfortable, ready for their interview.

b   _____ always making sure that all kitchen utensils are placed in the dishwasher before the last member of staff goes home.

c   If the utensils aren't washed, _____ not able to use them.

d   When setting out stationery, we always have everything laid out _____ it is in easy reach of the admin assistant.

e   When cutting paper, _____ always checking that each side is straight and contoured to level up with the other.

f   We make sure that any computer work is always carried out _____ there is good light.

g   Our receptionist always makes sure that she has plenty of time to deal with the recorded delivery mail and leaves it _____ the postman has easy access to it.

h   We always make sure that the customer has paid for parking when they come to a meeting; it would be awful if the customer _____ to get a parking ticket.

i   If we _____ not to offer any aftersales advice as part of the photocopying service, we would be providing a disservice to our customers.

j   _____ always happy when a customer recommends our services, as it shows that they _____ satisfied with the service they received.

QUESTION 4

The following chart relates to words that sound the same, but are spelt differently and have different meanings (homophones). Complete the chart, where applicable, providing clues for the word's meaning and/or a short sentence to put the word in the correct context.

Word	Clue for meaning	Short sentence
Hear	To listen to.	
Here	In this place.	
Weak		I felt so weak this morning, I could hardly move.
Week	A period of seven consecutive days.	
Piece		I'll only have a small piece of chocolate cake, thank you.
Peace	Freedom from strife, arguments or war.	
Cue		During the play, he spotted his cue to speak.
Queue	To form a line while waiting.	
Allowed		
Aloud		You're not meant to speak aloud in a library.
Knew	The past tense of 'know'.	
New		

Stationery	Writing materials such as pens, pencils, paper and envelopes.	
Stationary		Locking the castors on a stool makes it stationary.
Whole	The complete sum, amount or quantity of anything.	
Hole		I must have lost my money through the hole in my pocket.
Draught	A current of air, usually of a different temperature, entering an enclosed space.	
Draft	A first sketch, or version, of writing, which could be subject to revision.	
Draw		
Drawer	A lidless container that slides in and out of a chest or table.	

QUESTION 5

Which of these pairs of words are NOT homophones?

(1) hear / here

(2) write / right

(3) stop / cease

(4) new / knew

Answer:

Short-answer questions

Specific instructions to students

- The following questions relate to writing letters and emails.
- Read the questions carefully, then answer accordingly.

Task 1

QUESTION 1

Which type of letter is likely to be informal in style?

(1) Making an appointment to see the bank manager

(2) Confirming an interview date

(3) Email to a friend

(4) Making a complaint

Answer:

QUESTION 2

As well as thinking about the recipient of your letter or email, what else do you need to think about when writing a letter or email?

(1) The content

(2) The style

(3) The layout

(4) All of the above

Answer:

QUESTION 3

True or false? When writing an email, you need to select the email address of the person you want to receive it before selecting the 'send' button.

Answer:

QUESTION 4

How would you describe the 'content' of a letter or email?

(1) The formality with which you are writing

(2) The ideas and information you are writing

(3) The amount of text you are writing

Answer:

QUESTION 5

When sending an email, if you want other people to receive it but do not want to share their email addresses, which box would you select?

(1) 'Forward'

(2) 'Cc'

(3) 'Bcc'

(4) 'Send / Receive'

Answer:

Task 2

QUESTION 1

Parts a) to h) relate to this letter of complaint. Please read it carefully and refer to it to answer the questions.

Trumatter Solicitors Ltd

37 North Street

Millwharf

Ipswich

PE48 7ER

9 April 2013

The Manager

Total Photocopying Equipment for the 21st Century

Fenchurch Street

Leeds

LS17 3QQ

Dear Sir or Madam

1   Your office contacted me on 15 March regarding the urgent repairs that were required to the office
2   photocopier model HPT35902 which had been identified as representing a fire hazard. Your service
3   engineer carried out the necessary repairs on 29 March.

4   Within a day I noticed that the paper was scourcing hot and jamming each time a document needed
5   photocopying, so I cannot run the risk of using this piece of equipment. This has had the knock-
6   on effect of our being unable to deal with our daily schedule of cases, as each document must be
7   photocopied and filed, and we have lost potential earnings due to cases not being closed on the
8   scheduled date.

9   My colleagues and I rely heavily on the use of this photocopier and the loss of it has caused
10 us great inconvenience and loss of earnings. As none of this is our fault, I am appealing to you
11 to replace the photocopier and to reimburse the company for the loss of earnings which it has
12 incurred.

I hope to hear from you in the near future.

Yours sincerely

Bethany Lewis

Administrative Assistant

a What is wrong with the closing phrase at the end of the letter?

Answer:

_____

_____

b What does the word 'inconvenience' mean, in the third paragraph?

Answer:

_____

_____

c Which paragraph of the letter outlines the reason for the complaint?

Answer:

_____

d Line 4 contains a spelling error. What is the word and how should it be spelt?

Answer:

_____

e Which word or phrase, used in the letter, means 'to pay back'?

Answer:

_____

f What is the main complaint in this letter?

Answer:

_____

_____

g How would you describe the style of writing used by Bethany in her letter?

Answer:

_____

h In which paragraph of Bethany's letter does she use her most persuasive language?

Answer:

_____

Task 3

QUESTION 1

The following exercises contain a mixture of sentences that have either already been shortened, using apostrophes, or require shortening. Read them carefully, and then reword the sentence accordingly.

a Business Administrators should understand that they've got rights in the workplace.

Answer:

_____

_____

b Business Administrators should not disrespect the rights of other members of staff in the work place.

Answer:

_____

_____

c I've got responsibilities with regard to Health and Safety; however, I'll need to be trained.

Answer:

_____

_____

d I should not need much help with problems that arise at work as I have got a staff handbook.

Answer:

_____

_____

e It is only 10.30 a.m. and I cannot believe how hungry I am!

Answer:

_____

_____

f He would not believe that I had missed the last bus home.

Answer:

_____

_____

g She doesn't like to be absent from work as it puts too much pressure on other members of staff.

Answer:

_____

_____

QUESTION 2

If you are applying for a job, what do you not need to include?

(1) What qualifications and experience you have

(2) Your plans for the future

(3) How long it will take to commute

(4) Why you want to work for the company

Answer:

_____

QUESTION 3

Caroline has written in response to the advertisement that she spotted in the Wigan Daily Post shown below.

Business Administrator required for local solicitor.

Must have 2 years' experience.

Please send your CV and covering letter, to:

Paul Smith

Raven Solicitors

27 Bold Street

Wigan

She has asked you to look over her covering letter to see if she has included all the relevant points, before she posts it. She has also asked if you can help her write it again, if necessary.

Hi there

I want the job you've put in the local news paper this week. I've worked in Business Admin for 2 years and I can get people to vouch for me, if you want. Here's a list of my qualifications and where I've worked before, in with this letter.

You can call me on 07562 725094

Caroline

Help Caroline by rewriting the short covering letter to accompany her CV including the correct structure, content and layout for a formal covering letter.

Answer:

Task 4

The Administration Manager has dropped a memo in your tray asking you to complete a purchase order for computer supplies that she needs urgently (she assumes you have a price list). The items are as follows: cordless mouse, ergonomic keyboard, HP deskjet cartridge – black for a 690C inkjet printer, HP laserjet 5000 toner, mouse mat, wrist rest, screen clean wipes, aerosol duster for cleaning keyboards, foot rest and computer VDU filter.

PURCHASE ORDER

DATE:

PURCHASE ORDER:

CUSTOMER ID:

SHIP TO:

ITEM	AMOUNT

SUBTOTAL TO INCLUDE TAX

OTHER COMMENTS		
1. Total payment due in 10 days	SUBTOTAL	
	TAX	
	S&H	
	OTHER	
	TOTAL DUE	

If you have any questions about this purchase order, please contact the Administration Assistant.

Task 5: Email writing

Your colleague Jack Smith is retiring. You have been asked to organize a collection for a leaving gift, and to get people to sign a card.

You should mention:

- Who is retiring
- Why you are sending the email
- How people can give money and by when
- How they can sign the card

Remember:	Purpose
	Audience
	Content
	Tone

QUESTION 1

Write an email to your workmates to let them know about your colleague's retirement and the collection.

Answer:

QUESTION 2

The collection for your colleague has raised £90.00. You purchase a collection of gardening tools for Jack's leaving gift and a gift card.

Draft a note of the gift message.

Answer:

QUESTION 3

Send an email to the same workmates letting them know what you have purchased.

You should include:

- Thanks for their contributions
- How much was raised
- What gift you have chosen
- When the presentation will be made

Answer:

Task 6: Emailing at work

You work as a receptionist in a dental surgery. One of your daily tasks is to email the dentist a patient list for the day. You also email the dentist, Mr Makan, to tell him when his patients arrive. Look at these examples:

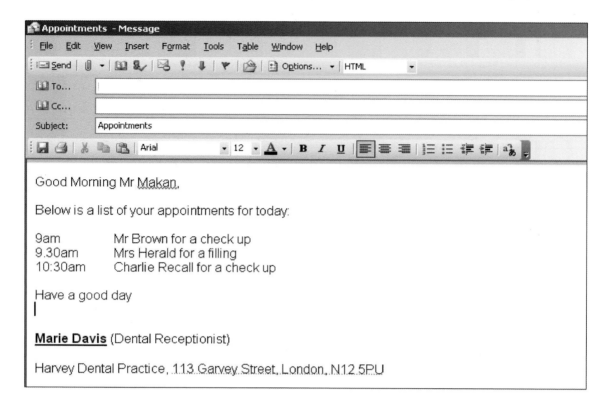

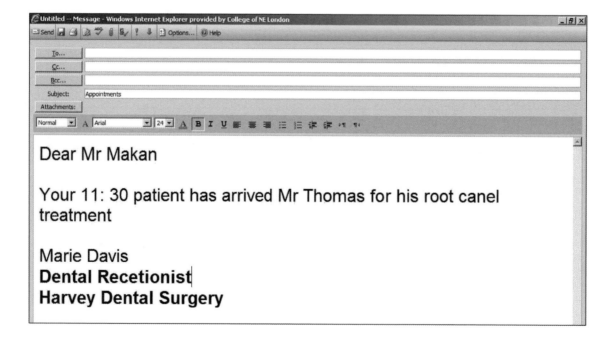

- You will need a copy of the Appointment Diary

- Please send a copy of all your emails to your tutor.

- Remember to do a spell check before clicking send.

QUESTION 1

Compose a new email message letting Mr Makan know what appointments he has today. Include: the time, patient name and treatment (see example).

QUESTION 2

Send an email to Mr Makan letting him know the time and the name of his first appointment.

QUESTION 3

Send an email to Mr Makan letting him know that his 10.00 patient has arrived.

QUESTION 4

Send an email to Mr Makan letting him know that his 4 p.m. appointment has been cancelled.

Harvey Dental Practice
113 Garvey Street, London, N12 SPU

Appointment Diary – Mr Makan

	Name	Treatment
09.00	Mrs Smith	6 month check-up
09.30	Mr Langley	6 month check-up
10.00	Miss Perez	Tooth filling
10.30		
11.00	Miss Weekly	6 month check-up
11.30	Mr Thomas	Root canal
12.00		
12.30		
13.00	LUNCH	
13.30	LUNCH	
14.00	Mr Pond	Tooth extraction
14.30		
15.00		
15.30	Mrs Roberts	6 month check-up
16.00	Miss Bennett	6 month check-up

Surgery Closed

Opening hours

Monday: closed

Tuesday–Friday: 9 a.m.–4 p.m.

Saturday: emergencies only

MATHEMATICS

It is important to show your workings to indicate how you calculated your answer. Use this workbook to practice the questions and record your answers. Use the blank Notes pages at the back of this book to record your workings.

Unit 7: General Mathematics

Short-answer questions

Specific instructions to students

- This unit will help you to improve your general mathematical skills.
- Read the following questions and answer all of them in the spaces provided.
- You need to show all working. Use the blank Notes pages at the back of this book.

QUESTION 1

What unit of measurement would you use to measure:

a The length of a desktop?

Answer:

_____

b The temperature of air conditioning?

Answer:

_____

c The amount of money in petty cash?

Answer:

_____

d The weight of a receptionist's chair?

Answer:

_____

e The voltage of an appliance (such as a coffee maker)?

Answer:

_____

QUESTION 2

Write an example of the following and where it may be used in business administration:

a Percentages

Answer:

_____

b Decimals

Answer:

_____

c Fractions

Answer:

_____

d Mixed numbers

Answer:

_____

e Ratios

Answer:

_____

_____

f Angles

Answer:

_____

_____

QUESTION 3
Convert the following units:

a   12 kg to grams

Answer:

_____

b   4 tonnes to kilograms

Answer:

_____

c   120 cm to metres

Answer:

_____

d   1140 ml to litres

Answer:

_____

e   1650 g to kilograms

Answer:

_____

f   1880 kg to tonnes

Answer:

_____

g   13 m to centimetres

Answer:

_____

h   4.5 litres to millilitres

Answer:

_____

QUESTION 4
Write the following in descending order:

0.4   0.04   4.1   40.0   400.00   4.0

Answer:

_____

QUESTION 5
Write the decimal number that is halfway between the following:

a   0.2 and 0.4

Answer:

_____

b   1.8 and 1.9

Answer:

_____

c   12.4 and 12.5

Answer:

_____

d   28.3 and 28.4

Answer:

_____

e   101.5 and 101.7

Answer:

_____

QUESTION 6
Round off the following numbers to two decimal places:

a   12.346

Answer:

_____

b   2.251

Answer:

_____

c   123.897

Answer:

_____

d   688.882

Answer:

_____

e   1209.741

Answer:

_____

QUESTION 7

Estimate the following by approximation:

a $1288 \times 19 =$

Answer:

b $201 \times 20 =$

Answer:

c $497 \times 12.2 =$

Answer:

d $1008 \times 10.3 =$

Answer:

e $399 \times 22 =$

Answer:

f $201 - 19 =$

Answer:

g $502 - 61 =$

Answer:

h $1003 - 49 =$

Answer:

i $10\,001 - 199 =$

Answer:

j $99.99 - 39.8 =$

Answer:

QUESTION 8

What do the following add up to?

a £4, £4.99 and £144.95

Answer:

b 8.75, 6.9 and 12.55

Answer:

c 65 ml, 18 ml and 209 ml

Answer:

d 21.3 g, 119 g and 884.65 g

Answer:

QUESTION 9

Subtract the following:

a 2338 from 7117

Answer:

b 1786 from 3112

Answer:

c 5979 from 8014

Answer:

d 11 989 from 26 221

Answer:

e 108 767 from 231 111

Answer:

QUESTION 10

Use division to solve the following:

a $2177 \div 7 =$

Answer:

_____

b $4484 \div 4 =$

Answer:

_____

c $63.9 \div 0.3 =$

Answer:

_____

d $121.63 \div 1.2 =$

Answer:

_____

e $466.88 \div 0.8 =$

Answer:

_____

QUESTION 11

Ratios:

a   One morning a postman delivered 42 first class
letters and 48 second class letters. What is the ratio
of the numbers of first class letters to the number of
second class letters?

Answer:

_____

b   In a business, it takes 55 minutes to deal with an
Internet order and 1 hour and 5 minutes to deal with
a telephone order. What is the ratio of the time an
Internet order takes to the time a telephone order
takes?

Answer:

_____

c   A 75 centilitre carton of orange juice contains enough
orange juice to fill six small glasses at the conference.
How many small glasses will three one-litre cartons
fill? (1 litre = 100 cl)

Answer:

_____

d   A fruit punch at the office summer party is made
from orange juice, cranberry juice and mango juice
in the ratio 5 : 4 : 1. How much cranberry juice will
there be in a 250 ml glass of fruit punch?

Answer:

_____

e   Two business administrators share the weekly
rent on their flat in the ratio 5 : 4. The weekly
rent is £90.00. How much does the first business
administrator pay?

Answer:

_____

f   A scale diagram of an office shows the width of the
office as 6.5 cm. The scale is 1 : 200. What is the real
width of the office, in metres?

Answer:

_____

The following information is provided for Question 12.

To solve using BODMAS, in order from left to right,
solve the Brackets first, then Order ('to the power of'),
then Division, then Multiplication, then Addition and
lastly Subtraction. The following example has been done
for your reference.

EXAMPLE :

Solve $(4 \times 7) \times 2 + 6 - 4$.

STEP 1

Solve the Brackets first: $(4 \times 7) = 28$

STEP 2

No Division so next solve Multiplication: $28 \times 2 = 56$

STEP 3

Addition is next: $56 + 6 = 62$

STEP 4

Subtraction is the last process: $62 - 4 = 58$

FINAL ANSWER

QUESTION 12

Using the acronym BODMAS, solve:

a $(6 \times 9) \times 5 + 7 - 2 =$

Answer:

b $(9 \times 8) \times 4 + 6 - 1 =$

Answer:

c $3 \times (5 \times 7) + 11 - 8 =$

Answer:

d $5 \times (8 \times 3) + 9 - 6 =$

Answer:

e $7 + 6 \times 3 + (9 \times 6) - 9 =$

Answer:

f $6 + 9 \times 4 + (6 \times 7) - 21 =$

Answer:

Section A: Addition

Short-answer questions

Specific instructions to students

- This section will help you to improve your addition skills for basic operations.
- Read the questions below and answer all of them in the spaces provided.
- You need to show all working, you can use the blank Notes pages at the back of this book.

QUESTION 1

A receptionist tends to three petty cash vouchers. The vouchers are for 2 l of milk costing £3, a jar of coffee costing £8 and a packet of biscuits for £5. What would the total be?

Answer:

QUESTION 2

Four petty cash vouchers contain the following details: stationery costing £60, postage stamps totalling £18, envelopes costing £12 and sandwiches for a lunch costing £50. What is the total?

Answer:

QUESTION 3

A front office does a stocktake and finds the following items in stock: 127 pens, 26 manila folders and 32 binders. How many items are in stock, in total?

Answer:

QUESTION 4

An administration assistant purchases the following for the office: cleaning products for £35, coffee, tea and sugar for £45, envelopes for £17 and a box of staples, paper clips and a hole punch for £19. How much has been spent in total?

Answer:

QUESTION 5

An administrative assistant takes the following amount of time to file documents: employee personal details – 13 minutes, medical files – 14 minutes, patient files – 17 minutes and Medicare documents – 23 minutes.

a   How much time has been taken, in minutes?

Answer:

b   How much time has been taken in hours and minutes?

Answer:

QUESTION 6

A receptionist purchases the following items: three binders for £25, two jars of coffee for £35, 10 bottles of purified water for £45 and 20 display folders for £25. How much money has been spent?

Answer:

QUESTION 7

An employee submits the following vouchers to the receptionist for reimbursement after a day's conference: two vouchers for taxi fares totalling £115, food costing £25, drinks with staff from other companies for £89 and the fee to attend the conference paid on the day costing £65. How much is the total reimbursement?

Answer:

QUESTION 8

On Friday, the receptionist balances cash in the petty cash box. The box has 2 × £50 notes, 4 × £20 notes, 3 × £10 notes, 9 × £5 notes, 12 × £2 coins and 11 × £1 coins. What is the total?

Answer:

QUESTION 9

An administrative assistant is asked to balance the following amounts of cash and coin that has been received by a small company: 6 × £50 notes, 9 × £20 notes, 15 × £10 notes, 19 × £5 notes, 26 × £2 coins and 38 × £1 coins. What is the total?

Answer:

QUESTION 10

A company has been fundraising for a charity. The following amounts are received and need to be counted: 5 × £50 notes, 22 × £20 notes, 133 × £10 notes, 14 × £5 notes, 129 × £2 coins and 163 × £1 coins. How much did the company raise for the charity?

Answer:

Section B: Subtraction

QUESTION 1

An office purchases a range of stationary that costs £12. How much change is given from £50?

Answer:

_____

QUESTION 2

Four document wallets and a box of overhead transparency sheets are bought for an office at a cost of £43. How much change will be given from £100?

Answer:

_____

QUESTION 3

A receptionist purchases the following office supplies: five packets of AAA batteries for £9, 24 whiteboard markers for £41 and six glue sticks for £15. How much change will be given from £100?

Answer:

_____

QUESTION 4

An office uses 27 whiteboard markers from a box that contains 100 whiteboard markers. How many are left in the box?

Answer:

_____

QUESTION 5

The total cost of office supplies for the period of January to June comes to £425. The bill is paid from petty cash using 10 × £50 notes. How much change should be received?

Answer:

QUESTION 6

A company uses 31 display folders from a box that contains 50 display folders. How many are left in the box?

Answer:

QUESTION 7

A lunch for management costs £135. The receptionist pays for it from petty cash using three £50 notes. How much change will he receive?

Answer:

QUESTION 8

An administrative assistant purchases stock for a paper company. The total cost comes to £68. Two £50 notes are used from petty cash to pay for the purchases. How much change is received?

Answer:

QUESTION 9

A receptionist purchases the following items for the office: 12 AA batteries for £9, six packets of staples for £7 and 10 whiteboard markers for £17. If there was £211 in the petty cash box before paying for the purchases, how much money remains after payment is completed?

Answer:

QUESTION 10

An office purchases 24 display folders for £34, two pads of graph paper for £5, five glue sticks for £11 and 50 whiteboard markers of various colours for £85. If there was £302 in petty cash prior to the purchases, how much will be left after the purchases?

Answer:

Section C: Multiplication

Task 1 🔵

Short-answer questions

Specific instructions to students

- This section will help you to improve your multiplication skills for basic operations.
- Read the following questions and answer all of them in the spaces provided.
- You need to show all working, you can use the blank Notes pages at the back of this book.

QUESTION 1

If document wallets cost £3 each, how much would 25 document wallets cost?

Answer:

_____

QUESTION 2

If black pens cost £2 each, how much would 75 black pens cost?

Answer:

_____

QUESTION 3

Management order 4 lunches in a month for meetings. Each luncheon costs £37. What will the total cost be for a month?

Answer:

_____

QUESTION 4

Each month the cost for coffee, tea, milk and sugar comes to £28. What is the total cost for six months worth of these items?

Answer:

_____

QUESTION 5

Each month a set of documents need to be posted to a local company. Each time they are posted it costs £9. What would be the total expenditure for posting the items over a 15-month period?

Answer:

QUESTION 6

A group of seven visitors take two taxis to the city from the airport for a meeting. The cost for each taxi comes to £39. What is the total for both taxis?

Answer:

QUESTION 7

A cheque for £237 is made out each month to a cleaning company for cleaning the offices. How much is spent on cleaning for a year?

Answer:

QUESTION 8

A water filtration system for a large company requires servicing quarterly. Each service costs £65. How much does the administrative assistant make the cheque out for at the end of each financial year?

Answer:

QUESTION 9

Twelve new leather chairs are purchased for a company's boardroom. Each chair costs £185. How much will the total be?

Answer:

QUESTION 10

A receptionist purchases five coffee tables. If each one costs £87, how much will all five cost?

Answer:

Task 2: Multiplication L1

The manager of a charity shop is very busy and knows that you are studying for a Business Administration Qualification as you volunteer at the shop when you have time. He asks you to help with the stock.

There are piles of goods in the shop, listed below. Fill in the table with the total number of items and the total price (if all the items are sold).

Item	Price (each)	Number of piles	Number of items in each pile	Total number	Total price
Records	£1	13	40		
CDs	£3	20	45		
Jigsaws	£2	5	24		
Computer games	£5	11	26		
Knives and forks	£0.90	18	25 pairs		
Blue plates	£0.50	14	12		
Bone china cups	£0.80	15	4		
Hats	£1.20	12	15		

Section D: Division ⓛ

QUESTION 1

If five items of furniture are purchased for £110, how much will the unit cost be for each?

Answer:

QUESTION 2

If a receptionist earns £568 (before tax) for working a five-day week, how much would the receptionist earn per day?

Answer:

QUESTION 3

A purchasing officer purchases four chairs for an office and the total comes to £260. How much does each chair cost?

Answer:

QUESTION 4

A receptionist purchases eight AA batteries for £6. What is the unit cost?

Answer:

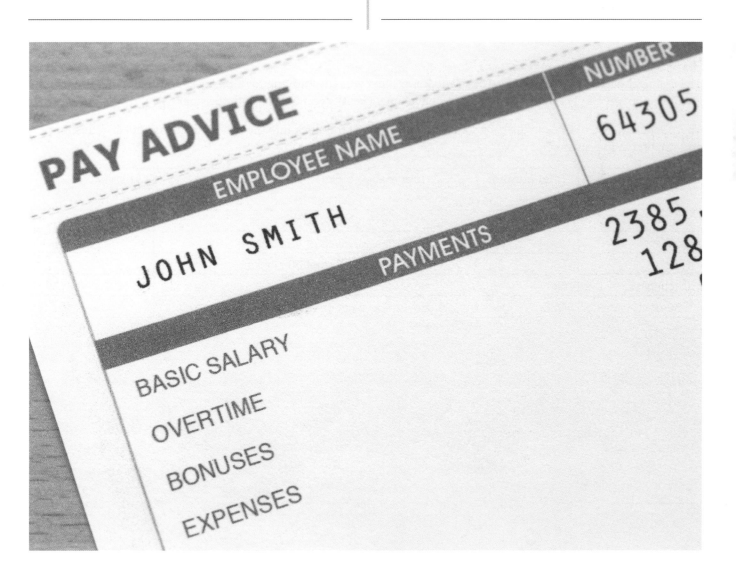

QUESTION 5

A company sends 12 documents using registered mail to a local company at a cost of £156. How much does each document cost to send?

Answer:

QUESTION 6

A company's income totals £15 699 for three weeks. What is the average weekly income for this period?

Answer:

QUESTION 7

A company spends £371 on seven lunches for meetings. How much does each lunch cost?

Answer:

QUESTION 8

There are 36 people invited to the opening of a new trade facility. Nibbles and drinks are provided for the visitors and the bill comes to £828. What is the cost per person?

Answer:

QUESTION 9

A company has 12 employees. The total of their wages comes to £390 000. What is the average wage per person?

Answer:

QUESTION 10

A company employs 20 workers. The total of their wages comes to £540 000. What is the average wage per worker?

Answer:

QUESTION 11

The manager of a charity shop is very busy and knows that you are studying for a Business Administration Qualification as you volunteer there when you have time. He asks you to help with the stock.

There is a huge pile of stock in the back room. You have to sort the stock into groups so the items appear refreshing and exciting to the customers.

Item	Total number	How many stacks?	Answer
Plates	260	How many stacks of 20 can you make?	
Socks	84 pairs	How many baskets with 6 pairs?	
Books	450	How many shelves of 45 books?	
Clocks	180	How many shelves of 30 clocks?	
Chocolates	640	How many piles of 40?	
Towels	400	How many piles of 20?	

Section A: Addition

Short-answer questions

Specific instructions to students

- This section will help you to improve your addition skills when working with decimals.
- Read the following questions and answer all of them in the spaces provided.
- You need to show all working, you can use the blank Notes pages at the back of this book.

QUESTION 1

If four 2 l bottles of milk are purchased for £14.80 and six bottles of liquid paper are purchased for £40.80, what is the total for the purchases?

Answer:

QUESTION 2

A receptionist purchases coffee for £22.95, tea for £18.95, sugar for £2.95 and a packet of biscuits for £6.95. How much has been spent?

Answer:

QUESTION 3

A new water cooler costs £62.50 and cups cost £13.95. How much does the order come to?

Answer:

QUESTION 4

A 12-pack of binders is purchased for £71.40 as well as six packets of staples for £10.50. How much is the total?

Answer:

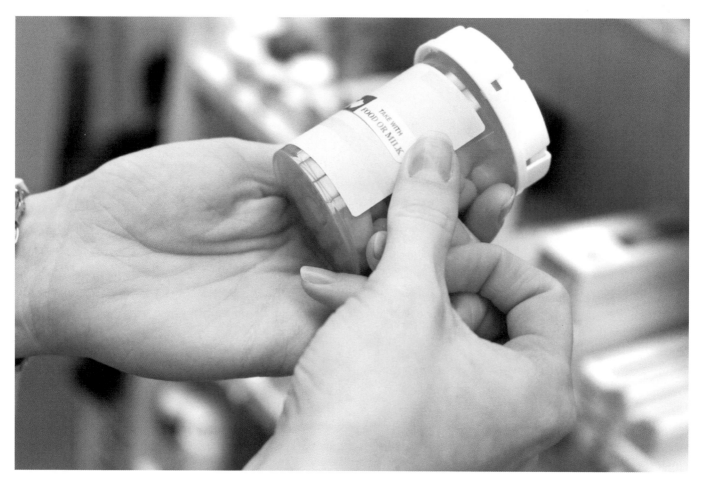

QUESTION 5

A company forwards documents by courier to three clients. The cost of the service to each client by the courier is £14.75, £8.95 and £21.50 respectively. How much is the total cost for forwarding the documents?

Answer:

QUESTION 6

A company receives cheques from four clients. The amount of each cheque is £220.50, £150.85, £135.50 and £189.90. How much do the cheques total?

Answer:

QUESTION 7

A receptionist purchases furniture for an office. The main table costs £345.50, four chairs cost £165.95 as a set and a coffee table is purchased for £59.95. What total should the cheque be made out for?

Answer:

QUESTION 8

Five patients at a dentist have different procedures. The cost of each procedure is £86.50, £135.50, £110.25, £347.90 and £1198.50. What will the total for all of the procedures come to?

Answer:

QUESTION 9

A medical receptionist receives four different items for use in the practice. All goods arrive separately. The items cost £78.90, £91.65, £160.45 and £359.95. What is the total cost of the receivable goods?

Answer:

QUESTION 10

A solicitor's practice charges six different clients the following fees: £889.90, £945.50, £1555.50, £2135.50, £732.50 and £569.25. What is the total of the fees?

Answer:

QUESTION 11

Mel goes to the department store and buys a pair of shoes costing £69.95, a coat at £79.99 and a hat at £12.50 for the staff outing to the races.

Answer:

Section B: Subtraction

QUESTION 1

A company purchases £18.65 worth of stationery. What change will be given from a £50 note from petty cash?

Answer:

QUESTION 2

An administrative assistant purchases 12 display folders for £21.60. What change will need to go back to petty cash if a £50 note was used to pay for the purchases?

Answer:

QUESTION 3

A part-time receptionist works 18 hours and earns £256.50. The receptionist uses £34.75 for petrol and £84.50 for nights out. How much is left?

Answer:

QUESTION 4

A building company pays cash for goods. The cost of the goods comes to £198.75. The petty cash box has a total of £313.15. What will the total of the petty cash be after the goods are paid for?

Answer:

QUESTION 5

A receptionist purchases a monthly magazine for their steel company from a newsagent. The cost comes to £114.50. The receptionist pays with three £50 notes. How much change is given?

Answer:

QUESTION 6

The members of a committee want to have a meeting, and drinks and food are to be supplied. The cost of the drinks and food comes to £87.50. There is £133.20 in petty cash. How much will be left once the drinks and food are paid for?

Answer:

QUESTION 7

A receptionist gets paid £568.50 for a week's work. If £178.50 is used to pay for a service on a car, £45.75 is paid for hairdressing and £126 is spent on nights out, how much money is left?

Answer:

QUESTION 8

A courier delivers two glass tables to a company and requires cash on delivery (COD). The total cost is £456.80. There is £512.40 in petty cash. Once the courier is paid, how much money remains in petty cash?

Answer:

QUESTION 9

Five workers at a screen printing business are paid the following fortnightly wages: £1112.75, £1135.95, £2111.75, £1875.90 and £1450.50. How much will be left in the payroll account, if there was £17 113.90 prior to payment of the wages?

Answer:

QUESTION 10

The Chief Executive of a drinks company is on a salary of £12 240 a month. If the amount in the payroll account for one month is £410 013, how much will be left after the Chief Executive receives the salary?

Answer:

QUESTION 11

Jake buys a Manchester United top and a scarf which all cost £30.99. He regularly goes to the matches with the Office Manager as they are both season ticket holders. He doesn't like the scarf which cost £6.49 and asks for a refund under the shop's 'no quibble' returns policy. How much has he spent after he's got his money back?

Answer:

Section C: Multiplication

QUESTION 1

If one stamp costs 50 pence, how much will a packet of 50 stamps cost?

Answer:

QUESTION 2

An office uses 38 black pens costing £0.95 each. How much will all 38 pens cost?

Answer:

QUESTION 3

A receptionist purchases three packets of 100 envelopes. If each packet costs £6.50, what is the total?

Answer:

QUESTION 4

An assistant manager purchases eight document folders that cost £6.95 each. How much is the total cost?

Answer:

QUESTION 5

An administrative assistant buys 24 manila folders that cost 90 pence each. What is the total cost?

Answer:

QUESTION 6

Six customers purchase goods from a toy company costing £35.50 each. What is the total?

Answer:

QUESTION 7

Thirteen customers purchase barbecues at a cost of £670.50 each. What would be the total?

Answer:

QUESTION 8

A wedding reception is held at a hotel. The cost per head is £75.50 and there will be 130 guests. How much will the total bill be?

Answer:

QUESTION 9

A group of 17 Year 12 students are preparing for a school trip. They all decide to stay in the same apartment block and they are offered a package deal by the management. The receptionist makes the booking. The cost per student for the week is £790.90 plus a booking fee of £8.50 per student.

a How much will the total bill be per student, including the booking fee?

Answer:

b How much will the total bill be for the whole group, including the booking fee?

Answer:

QUESTION 10

Twenty-five senior citizens treat themselves to a five-night trip to North Wales. They book a hotel that charges £92.50 per night. The booking fee is £6.50 per person.

a   How much does the receptionist charge per person, including the booking fee?

Answer:

_____

b   How much for the whole group, including the booking fee?

Answer:

_____

QUESTION 11

Mrs Jones decides to share the cost of her summer party between the 17 people from the office who have said they will come. She charges each guest £4.44 to cover the all of the costs, including the marquee, food and entertainment. How much will the party cost in total?

Answer:

_____

QUESTION 12

Max loves fresh coffee.

He drinks two mugs of coffee each day.

His favourite is Colombian.

He uses one-cup coffee filters, which are convenient. You just pour in boiling water and wait for it to drip through the coffee filter. Then you throw the filter away.

a   He spends £0.22 per filter. How much does it cost him in a five-day working week for his coffee?

Answer:

_____

He decides he is spending too much money on his coffee. Also, he is not happy about throwing away a lot of waste.

He buys a one-cup filter that can be used over and over again. He has to wash it after using it but that does not take long.

He buys a bag of coffee to use with this reusable filter. The bag contains 454 g of coffee.

It costs £4.69.

He puts two scoopfuls of this coffee in the filter to make one mug of coffee.

The two scoopfuls of coffee weigh about 14 g together.

b   How many mugs of coffee can he make with this bag?

Answer:

_____

_____

c   How many bags of this coffee would Max need to buy to last him a year?

Answer:

_____

_____

_____

Section D: Division

Short-answer questions

Specific instructions to students

- This section will help you to improve your division skills when working with decimals.
- Read the following questions and answer all of them in the spaces provided.
- You need to show all working, you can use the blank Notes page at the back of this book.

QUESTION 1

A box contains 24 manila folders which are distributed evenly to eight customers for their documents. How many folders does each customer receive?

Answer:

QUESTION 2

A receptionist earns £590.60 for a five-day week. How much is earned per day?

Answer:

QUESTION 3

In a medical clinic, there are 183 folders containing patients' information, which are divided evenly between three filing cabinets. How many will be filed in each cabinet?

Answer:

QUESTION 4

A receptionist working at a wholesale firm needs to allocate money evenly to three events: the Easter show, a mid-year conference and the Christmas show. The management budgets £11 530 for the three events and wants the money distributed evenly. How much does each event get allocated?

Answer:

QUESTION 5

An office assistant working at a roofing factory is asked to purchase eight platters of finger food for a luncheon. The assistant has £140 budgeted for the platters. How much will be allocated for each platter?

Answer:

QUESTION 6

A metal fabrication company is planning to hire two workers. Eight people apply for the two positions and management wants to interview the applicants between 9.00 a.m. and 11.00 a.m. only. How much time does the administrative assistant allocate for each interview if they all have the same amount of interview time?

Answer:

QUESTION 7

A printing company spends £113 on milk, coffee, sugar and tea over 4 weeks. What is the overall weekly expenditure for these items?

Answer:

QUESTION 8

A law firm sends eight documents to customers using registered post and the total bill comes to £98. How much, on average, does it cost to send each document?

Answer:

QUESTION 9

Over a month, a travel agency has sales totalling £112 850. What are the average weekly sales?

Answer:

QUESTION 10

A school budgets £211.50 for anti-bullying posters for nine Year 8 classrooms at the beginning of the year. How much money is allocated to each classroom for the posters?

Answer:

Section A: Addition 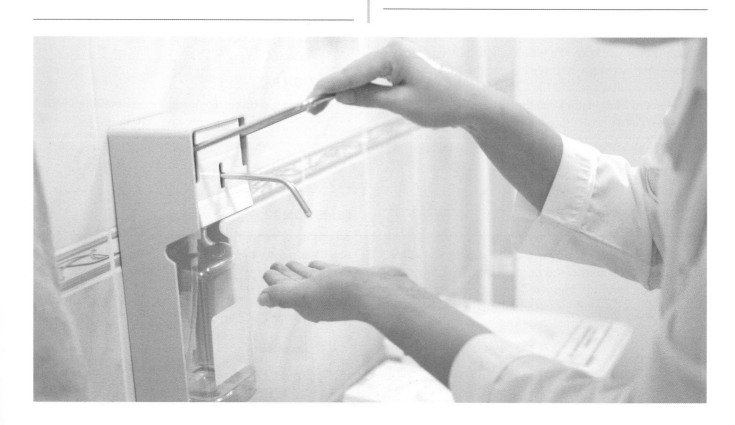(L1)

Short-answer questions

Specific instructions to students

- This section is designed to help you to improve your addition skills when working with fractions.
- Read the following questions and answer all of them in the spaces provided.
- You need to show all working, you can use the blank Notes page at the back of this book.

QUESTION 1

$\frac{1}{2} + \frac{4}{5} =$

Answer:

QUESTION 2

$2\frac{2}{4} + 1\frac{2}{3} =$

Answer:

QUESTION 3

An office worker in a medical clinic has three bottles of hand-sanitising lotion that must be divided into four containers. As a fraction, how much will go into each of the four containers?

Answer:

QUESTION 4

A receptionist needs to prepare an invoice for a customer and the number of hours spent on two automotive jobs needs to be calculated. If a mechanic has spent $1\frac{3}{4}$ hours working on one car and $\frac{3}{4}$ of an hour on another car, use fractions to calculate the total time taken on both cars.

Answer:

QUESTION 5

An office assistant spends $1\frac{1}{2}$ hours assisting with a corporate presentation and $1\frac{3}{4}$ hours preparing, sending and recording invoices for work completed by the company. How much time is spent on these two tasks?

Answer:

Section B: Subtraction

QUESTION 1

$\frac{2}{3} - \frac{1}{4} =$

Answer:

QUESTION 2

$2\frac{2}{3} - 1\frac{1}{4} =$

Answer:

QUESTION 3

A shop assistant has a shelf that is $\frac{2}{3}$ full of toys. If she removes $\frac{1}{3}$ of the toys from the shelf, how much room is left? Express your answer as a fraction.

Answer:

QUESTION 4

A newsagent has a shelf that is $\frac{1}{2}$ full of lifestyle magazines. If $\frac{1}{3}$ of the magazines are removed from the shelf, as they are out of date, how much of the shelf is left? Express your answer as a fraction.

Answer:

QUESTION 5

A shop assistant working in a café uses $1\frac{1}{3}$ cartons of milk on Monday to serve customers. A further $2\frac{1}{4}$ cartons of milk are used over Tuesday and Wednesday. How much milk is left in the open carton? Express your answer as a fraction.

Answer:

Section C: Multiplication

Short-answer questions

Specific instructions to students

- This section is designed to help you to improve your multiplication skills when working with fractions.
- Read the following questions and answer all of them in the spaces provided.
- You need to show all working, you can use the blank Notes at the back of the book.

QUESTION 1

$\frac{2}{4} \times \frac{2}{3} =$

Answer:

QUESTION 2

$2\frac{2}{3} \times 1\frac{1}{2} =$

Answer:

QUESTION 3

An office assistant spends $\frac{3}{4}$ of an hour each day on data entry for noting absentees at a school. If this task is undertaken each school day, use fractions to calculate the total time taken on data entry for a week.

Answer:

QUESTION 4

A travel agent takes $1\frac{1}{2}$ hours each day to research travelling in Europe. If the travel agent works six days each week, use fractions to calculate the total amount of time that is spent on this task.

Answer:

QUESTION 5

An administrative assistant spends $2\frac{1}{2}$ hours each week on organising and calculating the payroll for a major bus manufacturing company. Use fractions to calculate how much time is spent on this task each month.

Answer:

Section D: Division

QUESTION 1

$\frac{2}{3} \div \frac{1}{4} =$

Answer:

QUESTION 2

$2\frac{3}{4} \div 1\frac{1}{3} =$

Answer:

QUESTION 3

A receptionist takes $\frac{1}{4}$ of an hour to update and file one patient's medical records. How many records could be updated and filed in four hours?

Answer:

QUESTION 4

A school assistant has three empty bottles and two full bottles of hand lotion. The hand lotion needs to be transferred from the two full bottles to the three empty bottles evenly. As a fraction, how much hand lotion will be evenly transferred to each of the three empty bottles from the two full bottles?

Answer:

QUESTION 5

A car company is hosting a golf day and the receptionist is asked to assist. If there are two full bottles of sunscreen that need to be poured into six empty bottles, how much will be poured into each of the six empty bottles, as a fraction?

Answer:

Section E: Ratio, scale and proportion

QUESTION 1

The label on a large bottle of squash in the supermarket where you work states 'dilute 1 part squash to 3 parts water'. How much water must be added to 2 litres of squash?

(1) 0.5 litres

(2) 1.5 litres

(3) 6 litres

(4) 8 litres

Answer:

QUESTION 2

This recipe is for 4 fruit scones:

200 g flour

2 eggs

50 g butter

100 ml milk

50 g currants

How much flour would be needed to make 6 of these fruit scones?

(1) 30 g

(2) 300 g

(3) 400 g

(4) 1200 g

Answer:

QUESTION 3

A stall holder is making muffins to sell at a village fair. His recipe makes 12 muffins.

300 g flour

1 level teaspoon baking powder

90 g sugar

250 ml milk

2 eggs

4 tablespoons sunflower oil

How much flour does he need to make 60 muffins?

(1) 150 g

(2) 1500 g

(3) 1800 g

(4) 18 000 g

Answer:

QUESTION 4

Due to falling profit, 600 shop workers lose their jobs. 480 of these are women. What is the ratio of men to women who lose their jobs?

(1) 1 : 5

(2) 1 : 4

(3) 4 : 1

(4) 5 : 1

Answer:

QUESTION 5

A pool attendant adds chemicals to the pool each day. He mixes chemicals labelled 'Fresh' and 'Safe' in a ratio of 3 : 2. How much 'Fresh' is there in one litre of mixture?

(1) $\frac{2}{5}$ litre (2) $\frac{3}{5}$ litre

(3) $\frac{5}{3}$ litre (4) $\frac{3}{2}$ litre

Answer:

QUESTION 6

A man lives 1 km from a butchers shop. It takes him 15 minutes to walk to the shop. His walking speed is

(1) 4 metres per minute

(2) 4 kilometres per minute

(3) 4 metres per hour

(4) 4 kilometres per hour

Answer:

_____

QUESTION 7

Jane and Tom spend £5 between them on their lottery tickets each week at work. Jane puts in £1 and Tom puts in £4. They have agreed to share the winnings according to the amount they put in. One week they win £45 000. How much will they get each?

(1) Jane will get £15 000 and Tom will get £30 000

(2) Jane will get £11 000 and Tom will get £34 000

(3) Jane will get £10 000 and Tom will get £35 000

(4) Jane will get £9000 and Tom will get £36 000

Answer:

_____

QUESTION 8

Lee has a recipe for fruit punch which makes 15 glasses. Lee decides to make just enough fruit punch for 75 glasses. Recipe:

500 ml orange juice

500 ml pineapple juice

50 ml lemon juice

1 l sparkling water

How many millilitres (ml) of lemon juice will he need?

(1) 50 ml

(2) 75 ml

(3) 250 ml

(4) 500 ml

Answer:

_____

QUESTION 9

The British Heart Foundation recommends that children between the ages of 5 and 18 should spend at least an hour a day doing something active. Yet their research shows that one in three do not get nearly enough exercise. As a ratio is this:

(1) 1 : 3

(2) 1 : 2

(3) 1 : 4

(4) 1 : 1

Answer:

_____

QUESTION 10

A college decides to take 20 students on a retail trip. For safety, the ratio of adults to students must be at least 1 : 4. How many adults are required for safety?

(1) 1

(2) 4

(3) 5

(4) 6

Answer:

_____

QUESTION 11

The entire group (adults and students) goes to the shopping centre in cars. Each car is driven by an extra volunteer and can hold 4 passengers. How many cars would they need altogether?

(1) 5

(2) 6

(3) 7

(4) 10

Answer:

_____

QUESTION 12

Try converting a home-size recipe into restaurant size!

If a home-size recipe uses three-quarters of a teaspoon of a spice how many teaspoons of the spice would be needed for 10 times the quantity?

(1) 8 teaspoons

(2) 6.5 teaspoons

(3) 5 teaspoons

(4) 7.5 teaspoons

Answer:

_____

QUESTION 13

You are making some dishes for a 'Different Foods' week at work.

Spanish Flan (serves 8)

260 g sugar

60 ml water

10 ml vanilla essence

400 ml milk

260 ml whipping cream

6 eggs

2 egg yolks

a What is the ratio of water : vanilla essence in its simplest form? Show your working.

Answer:

_____

b Write out the recipe for 4 people.

Answer:

_____

_____

c How much water is needed for a larger flan that uses 600 ml milk? Show your working.

Answer:

_____

QUESTION 14

Dominique makes purple paint by mixing blue and red paint in the ratio 1 : 3 for painting the training room.

a How much red paint does she use with 2 tins of blue paint? Show your working.

Answer:

_____

b How much blue paint does she use with 12 tins of red paint? Show your working.

Answer:

_____

QUESTION 15

Simon makes fruit punch by mixing orange juice and mango juice the ratio 3 : 2 for the staff room party.

a How much mango juice does he mix with 6 litres orange juice? Show your working.

Answer:

_____

_____

b How much orange juice does he mix with 10 litres mango juice? Show your working.

Answer:

_____

_____

QUESTION 16

A recipe for risotto uses 300 g rice. The recipe is for 4 people.

a How much rice is needed for 8 people? Show your working.

Answer:

_____

b How much rice is needed for 20 people? Show your working.

Answer:

_____

c How much rice is needed for 2 people?

Answer:

_____

QUESTION 17

A recipe for soup uses 450 g parsnips. The recipe is for 6 people.

a What weight of parsnips is needed to make soup for 12 people? Show your working.

Answer:

_____

b What weight of parsnips is needed to make soup for 4 people? Show your working.

Answer:

_____

_____

QUESTION 18

Sarah is paid £40 for 5 hours work as a Administrative Assistant.

a   How much is she paid for 10 hours' work? Show your working.

Answer:

_____

b   How much is she paid for 1 hour's work? Show your working.

Answer:

_____

c   How much is she paid for 3 hours' work? Show your working.

Answer:

_____

QUESTION 19

Karim works from Monday to Friday each week. He is paid £245 a week. He works from 9 a.m. to 5 p.m. each day as a lorry driver with an hour (unpaid) for lunch.

a   How much does he earn per day? Show your working.

Answer:

_____

b   How much does he earn per hour? Show your working.

Answer:

_____

QUESTION 20

A large map of Europe has a scale of 1 : 600 000. Calculate the actual distance, in km, that the following lengths on the map represent.

a   1 cm. Show your working.

Answer:

_____

b   20 cm. Show your working.

Answer:

_____

QUESTION 21

You are taking your holidays from work to go to Budapest and Warsaw. The actual distance between two cities, Budapest and Warsaw is 600 km. What is the distance between these two cities on the map? Show your working.

Answer:

_____

_____

_____

Unit 11: Percentages L1

Short-answer questions

Specific instructions to students

- In this unit, you will be able to practise and improve your skills in working out percentages and ratios.
- Read the following questions and answer all of them in the spaces provided.
- You need to show all working, you can use the blank Notes pages at the back of this book.

10% rule: Move the decimal one place to the left to get 10%.

EXAMPLE

10% of £45.00 would be £4.50

QUESTION 1

A receptionist buys stationery at an office supplies store for £22.00. There is a '10% off' sale on.

a   What will the discount be?

Answer:

---

b   What will the bill come to after the 10% is taken off?

Answer:

QUESTION 2

A hotel advertises that it will deduct 20% off the final cost of three nights' accommodation if people book at a certain time of the year. A receptionist takes a booking that totals £330.00.

a   How much will the discount be?

Answer:

---

b   What is the final total for the three nights of accommodation?

Answer:

QUESTION 3

A travel agency has a '30% off' sale on flights to Europe. An agent takes a booking for a flight that costs £1200.00.

a   How much will the discount be?

Answer:

---

b   What will be the final cost?

Answer:

QUESTION 4

A receptionist at a law firm buys three filing cabinets for the practice. The total price comes to £360.80. A 5% discount is given.

a   How much is the discount worth?

Answer:

---

b   What is the final total? (Hint: Find 10%, halve it then subtract it from the overall price.)

Answer:

QUESTION 5

A legal secretary purchases two sandwich platters for £12, a new desk for £63 and four chairs for £120 at a '20% off' sale.

a   How much is the total of the purchase?

Answer:

---

b   How much would a 20% discount be?

Answer:

---

c   What is the final cost after the discount?

Answer:

QUESTION 6

The following items are purchased for a hospital by the purchasing officer: 24 white sheets for £162, 15 sets of pillow covers for £187.50, 12 mattress covers for £312, two chairs for £32 and four vases for £56.

a   What is the total?

Answer:

_____

b   What would a 10% discount be?

Answer:

_____

c   What is the final cost after the discount?

Answer:

_____

QUESTION 7

A store offers '20% off' the price of any stationery as long as the customer spends at least £100. If a customer spent £105, how much would six binders originally costing £39 be after the discount?

Answer:

_____

QUESTION 8

A particular range of vertical files is discounted by 15%. The recommended retail price of 100 vertical files is £248.

a   How much will the discount be?

Answer:

_____

b   What is the final price?

Answer:

_____

QUESTION 9

A secretary needs to buy bottles of sanitized hand lotion for the toilets and bathrooms at work. The bottles are priced at £16.90 each. The store has a '20% off' sale on this item. What will the sale price be?

Answer:

_____

QUESTION 10

Several styles of folders are priced at £5.90 each. During a sale the product is sold at '30% off'. What will the selling price be?

Answer:

_____

Short-answer questions

Specific instructions to students

- This unit is designed to help you to improve your skills and increase your speed in converting one measurement into another and solving problems.
- Read the following questions and answer all of them in the spaces provided.
- You need to show all working, you can use the blank Notes pages at the back of this book.

QUESTION 1

How many millimetres are there in 1 cm?

Answer:

QUESTION 2

How many centimetres are there in 1 m?

Answer:

QUESTION 3

How many millimetres are there in 1 m?

Answer:

QUESTION 4

If two documents are allowed in each folder, how many documents would there be in 10 folders?

Answer:

QUESTION 5

How many millilitres are there in a 1.5 l bottle of hand lotion?

Answer:

QUESTION 6

A 3500 ml bottle of purified water makes up how many litres?

Answer:

QUESTION 7

An oak boardroom table weighs a quarter of a tonne. How many kilograms is that?

Answer:

QUESTION 8

A delivery truck weighs 2 t. How many kilograms is that?

Answer:

QUESTION 9

A truck weighs 4750 kg. How many tonnes is that?

Answer:

QUESTION 10

A warehouse floor measures 4.8 m wide and 12 m long. How far is it around the perimeter of the warehouse?

Answer:

QUESTION 11

Convert 2 inches into centimetres.

Answer:

QUESTION 12

Convert 3 inches into centimetres.

Answer:

QUESTION 13

Convert 4 inches into centimetres.

Answer:

QUESTION 14

Convert 5 inches into centimetres.

Answer:

QUESTION 15

Convert $3\frac{1}{2}$ inches into centimetres.

Answer:

QUESTION 16

Convert 5 cm into inches.

Answer:

QUESTION 17

Convert 10 cm into inches.

Answer:

QUESTION 18

Convert 50 cm into inches.

Answer:

QUESTION 19

Convert 12.5 cm into inches.

Answer:

QUESTION 20

Convert 2.5 cm into inches.

Answer:

Distance		
1 inch	= 2.54 centimetres	= 25.4 millimetres
1 foot	= 0.305 metre	= 30.5 centimetres
1 yard	= 0.9244 metre	
1 mile	= 1.61 kilometres	= 5.280 feet
1 kilometre	= 1000 metres	= 0.6214 mile
1 metre	= 100 centimetres	= 1000 millimetres
1 metre	= 3.28 feet	
1 centimetre	= 0.3937 inch	= 10 millimetres
1 millimetre	= 0.039 inch	= 0.1 centimetre
1 micron	= 10^{-4} centimetre	= 10^{-5} metre
10^{-6} metre	= 1 micrometre	
Volume		
1 kilolitre	= 1000 litres	= 1 cubic metre
1 litre	= 1000 millilitres	= 1000 cc
1 millilitre	= 1 cc (exactly 1.000027 cc)	
1 fluid ounce	= 29.57 millilitres	
1 US gallon	= 3.785 litres	
1 Imperial gallon	= 4.546 litres	
Weight		
1 kilogram	= 1000 grams	= 2.2 pounds
1 gram	= 1000 milligrams	= 0.035 ounce
1 milligram	= 1000 micrograms	= 0.001 gram
1 microgram	= 10^{-6} grams	= 0.001 milligram
1 nanogram	= 10^{-9} grams	= 0.001 microgram
1 pound	= 0.45 kilogram	= 16 ounces
1 ounce	= 28.35 grams	

Task: French trip

On 30 July, Kim and her friend Jane bought 600 euros in Go Travel to spend on a holiday in France. They took Kim's car and used the Eurotunnel between Folkestone in the UK and Calais in France.

They are now in Calais on their way back home with 140.65 of the euros they bought. They want to treat themselves to a special lunch before they go back. Information about euros and lunch prices is given below.

EURO BANKNOTES

Euro notes are identical across the euro area.

They are in €500, €200, €100, €50, €20, €10 and €5 denominations.

They can be used anywhere within the euro area, regardless of country of issue. Each denomination has a different size and colour.

The values are printed in large figures to help the visually impaired recognize them.

EURO COINS

The coins are in 1, 2, 5, 10, 20 and 50 euro cent denominations and 1 and 2 euro denominations.

They can be used anywhere within the euro area.

Each coin has the same front but may have different symbols on the back, depending on where it was minted.

Go Travel

30 July

We only buy and sell euro banknotes.

We buy euros at €1.2526 for £1

We sell euros at €1.1156 for £1

Au Côte d'Argent

MENU DOUCEUR €18
(service included)

Home made fish soup

or

Fillet of herring with warm potatoes
and vinaigrette

or

Home made pate with piccalilli sauce

ɛᴏ ɛᴏ ɛᴏ

Stuffed leg of guinea fowl with cabbage

or

Fillet of salmon with pasta,
cream and chives

ɛᴏ ɛᴏ ɛᴏ

Dessert trolley

MENU DEUCE €25
(service included)

Seafood platter

or

Mussel soup with saffron

or

Burgundy snails with tomato sauce and
candied fennel

ɛᴏ ɛᴏ ɛᴏ

Fillet of cod and basil sauce

or

Fillet of salmon with mussels and green olives

or

Fillet of pork with stewed apple and
spring cabbage

ɛᴏ ɛᴏ ɛᴏ

Dessert trolley

QUESTION 1

Kim and Jane stop at the restaurant 'Au Côte d'Argent' in Calais. They both choose the *menu douceur*.

They drink tap water and have a coffee at the end that costs them €1 each.

a   How much is the total bill in euros?

Answer:

_____

b   How much did they pay for those euros in the UK?

Answer:

_____

c   How many euros do they have left now?

Answer:

_____

QUESTION 2

When they get home they are going to change as many of their euros as they can back to sterling. Kim's petrol tank is nearly empty. Filling it up will take about 47 litres of petrol. The price of petrol in Folkestone in the UK is 102.9p per litre. Where they are in Calais it costs €1.224 per litre.

Do you think they should fill up the tank in Calais or Folkestone? Explain your answer carefully. State clearly any assumptions you make.

Answer:

Short-answer questions

Specific instructions to students

- This unit will help you to calculate how much a service is worth and how long you need to complete the service.
- Read the following questions and answer all of them in the spaces provided.
- You need to show all working, you can use the blank Notes pages at the back of this book.

QUESTION 1

A part-time receptionist earns £360.60 net (take home per week). How much does this person earn per year if this is the regular weekly salary? (Remember, there are 52 weeks a year.)

Answer:

QUESTION 2

Susan is a part-time accountant at a glass manufacturing company. She starts work at 8.00 a.m. and has a break at 10.30 a.m. for 20 minutes. Lunch starts at 12.30 p.m. and finishes at 1.30 p.m. Then Susan works through to 4.00 p.m.

a   How long are the breaks in total?

Answer:

b   How many hours have been worked in total, excluding breaks?

Answer:

QUESTION 3

Linda works as a school assistant and earns £12.50 an hour. She works a 38-hour week. How much are her gross earnings per week (before tax)?

Answer:

QUESTION 4

Melissa is an administrative assistant and gets paid £411 net for her week's work. From this, she buys petrol which costs £36.95, jewellery worth £19.55, CDs worth £59.97 and a new dress that costs £57.50. She also spends £95 on nights out.

a   What is the total of all money spent?

Answer:

b   How much is left?

Answer:

QUESTION 5

Interviews for a new position at a law firm are conducted on a Monday morning. The interviews vary in length of time. One goes on for 34 minutes, whereas the others go for 18 minutes, 57 minutes, 44 minutes and 59 minutes respectively. How much time, in minutes and hours, has been taken for the interviews?

Answer:

QUESTION 6

A medical receptionist needs to collect, sort and file a number of patients' records. This takes the receptionist $1\frac{1}{4}$ hours to complete.

a   How many minutes is this?

Answer:

b How many hours are left, if the medical receptionist normally works an eight-hour day?

Answer:

_____

QUESTION 7

An assistant accountant needs to compile the weekly payroll which takes $1\frac{1}{2}$ hours to complete. Following this, work needs to be completed on data entry of stock which takes a further $1\frac{1}{4}$ hours.

a How many hours were spent on the two tasks? State your answer as a fraction.

Answer:

_____

b If the assistant accountant works an eight-hour day, how many hours are there left to work in the day, including breaks?

Answer:

_____

QUESTION 8

A receptionist prepares invoices for customers who have had electrical work completed. This takes the receptionist 1 hour 50 minutes to complete.

a How long, in hours and minutes, will be left in an eight-hour working day?

Answer:

_____

b How many minutes will the task take?

Answer:

_____

QUESTION 9

An administrative assistant begins work at 7.00 a.m. and works until 4.00 p.m. He takes a morning break for 20 minutes, a lunch break for 60 minutes and an afternoon break of 20 minutes.

a How much time has been spent on breaks?

Answer:

_____

b How much time has been spent working?

Answer:

_____

QUESTION 10

The invoice for work that has been completed by a screen-printing business comes to £1850.50. What would the hourly rate be if the workers had spent 10 hours on the work?

Answer:

_____

QUESTION 11

A buffet needs to be prepared in advance for a function. If it takes 3.5 hours to prepare the buffet, 1.5 hours to prepare and decorate the tables and $\frac{1}{2}$ hour to prepare drinks, how long has it taken in total?

Answer:

_____

QUESTION 12

Fill in the gaps on the timesheet below, using the following information.

Jane works a 5-hour shift.

Alison works for 4.5 hours.

Emma works for 6 hours and 45 minutes and gets paid £2.50 less than Alison.

Tania earns £1.75 more per hour than Jane and works for 7.5 hours with a half hour unpaid break in the middle of her shift.

Name	Time in	Time out	Rate of pay	Total
Jane	10.00		£6.50	
Alison		12.30	£10.45	£47.03
Abigail	7.45		£7.50	£33.75
Emma		16.00		
Tania	13.50			

Unit 14: Squaring Numbers

Section A: Introducing square numbers

Short-answer questions

Specific instructions to students

- This section is designed to help you to improve your skills and increase your speed in squaring numbers.
- Read the following questions and answer all of them in the spaces provided.
- You need to show all working, you can use the blank Notes pages at the back of this book.

Any number squared is multiplied by itself.

EXAMPLE

4 squared = 4^2 = 4 × 4 = 16

QUESTION 1

$6^2 =$

Answer:

QUESTION 2

$8^2 =$

Answer:

QUESTION 3

$12^2 =$

Answer:

QUESTION 4

$3^2 =$

Answer:

QUESTION 5

$7^2 =$

Answer:

QUESTION 6

$11^2 =$

Answer:

QUESTION 7

$10^2 =$

Answer:

QUESTION 8

$9^2 =$

Answer:

QUESTION 9

$2^2 =$

Answer:

QUESTION 10

$4^2 =$

Answer:

Section B: Applying square numbers to Business Administration

Worded practical problems

Specific instructions to students

- This section is designed to help you to improve your skills and increase your speed in calculating volumes of rectangular or square objects. The worded questions make the content relevant to everyday situations.
- Read the following questions and answer all of them in the spaces provided.
- You need to show all working, you can use the blank Notes pages at the back of this book.

QUESTION 1

If there are 5×5 vertical folders in a box, how many folders are there in total?

Answer:

QUESTION 2

Six packets of documents sent by registered post are received by a medical centre. If there are six documents in each packet, how many documents will there be in total?

Answer:

QUESTION 3

There are 12×12 liquid paper bottles packed into a box. How many bottles are in the box?

Answer:

QUESTION 4

A warehouse floor has an area that is 15 m $\times$ 15 m. How much floor area is this in square metres?

Answer:

QUESTION 5

A box contains colour samples for a textile company. The samples are in rows of 8×8. How many samples are there?

Answer:

QUESTION 6

A receptionist unpacks two boxes containing display items. The first box contains 4×4 company magazines. The second box contains 3×3 colour brochures for display. How many items are there in total?

Answer:

QUESTION 7

A box of new business cards is unpacked by a receptionist. If the cards are packed in a 20×20 formation, how many are there?

Answer:

QUESTION 8

An office stocks the following: 5×5 packets of black pens, 3×3 packets of pencils and 10×10 boxes of tissues. How many items of stock are there in total?

Answer:

QUESTION 9

The following items are stocked by a soft drink company and they need to be accounted for during a stocktake: 5×5 bottles of distilled water, 5×5 bottles of filtered water and 5×5 bottles of tonic water. How many bottles are there in total?

Answer:

QUESTION 10

The following items are listed during an office stocktake: 3×3 vertical files, 2×2 glue sticks, 2×2 blue pens and 3×3 black pens. How many single items are there in total?

Answer:

Short-answer questions

Specific instructions to students

- This unit will help you to calculate the details of invoices and bills.
- Read the following questions and answer all of them in the spaces provided.
- You need to show all working, you can use the blank Notes pages at the back of this book.

QUESTION 1

A customer makes an appointment to see a dentist. The total comes to £350.00. The dentist has had a promotion in the local paper that reduces the total cost of visits by 20% for one month only.

a   By how much does the dental receptionist need to adjust the final bill?

Answer:

b   How much will the final cost be?

Answer:

QUESTION 2

A customer books a trip with a travel agent. The customer receives a 10% discount due to a promotion that the travel agency is having.

a   If the trip costs £1275, how much will the travel agent need to take off due to the 10% discount?

Answer:

b   How much will the trip cost after the discount?

Answer:

QUESTION 3

A building company charges £65.50 as a call-out fee. The first hour is charged at £80. Each quarter hour after that is charged at £25. If the builder works for three hours, how much will the receptionist invoice the customer for?

Answer:

QUESTION 4

A client is charged for electrical work completed at their house. The call-out fee is £60. If the electrician takes two hours to install three lights and the hourly rate is £85, how much will the invoice be?

Answer:

QUESTION 5

A landscaping business charges £42 per hour per person for their services. If three landscapers spend $3\frac{1}{2}$ hours working in the back garden of a property, how much will the owner be charged?

Answer:

QUESTION 6

A company receives the following goods: masking tape for £12.60, a new printer for £145.00 and 50 vertical files with tabs for £39.95. A 15% voucher is included as a one-off special for an end-of-financial-year sale.

a   How much is the total before the discount?

Answer:

b   How much is the discount?

Answer:

c   What is the final cost?

Answer:

QUESTION 7

A hardware company purchases office supplies. The goods total £224. A '25% off' sale is on.

a How much is saved?

Answer:

_____

b What is the final cost?

Answer:

_____

QUESTION 8

Office furniture is purchased by an assistant manager for a small goods company. The total cost is £1121.50. A '10% off' voucher is used.

a How much is the voucher worth?

Answer:

_____

b What is the final cost?

Answer:

_____

QUESTION 9

Three different customers make purchases at an office supplies store. Each customer also has a '15% off' voucher. The first client purchases a hole punch, filing cabinets, pens, folders and envelopes, spending a total of £264. The second client purchases office furniture, masking tape, highlighter pens, whiteboard markers and vertical files for a total of £158. The third customer purchases graph books, lined books, a petty cash box, and manila and display folders, all for £88.

a How much is the total purchases for all three customers without the voucher?

Answer:

_____

b How much will the voucher decrease the cost for each customer?

Answer:

_____

_____

c What is the final cost for each of the three customers?

Answer:

_____

_____

d What is the total of the three customer's purchases after the discount?

Answer:

_____

QUESTION 10

Six friends book a holiday to Spain with the local travel agent. The six students book rooms at a hotel for six nights on the Costa Del Sol. The cost per person per night is £95. In addition, the six friends book a fishing trip for £68 per person and a skydiving experience for £235 per person. What will be the cost for each student?

Answer:

_____

Short-answer questions

Specific instructions to students

- The following questions will help you understand average, range, decimal places, format, style and how to collect and interpret data.
- Read the following questions, then answer accordingly.

The following questions relate to a vehicle hire business called Ajax. It is set in a busy town location where customers can hire a full range of vehicles from small cars to vans.

QUESTION 1

Ajax has included this diagram in its staff handbook, to show the staff structure. The next few questions are related to this diagram.

a   What is this type of diagram called?

Answer:

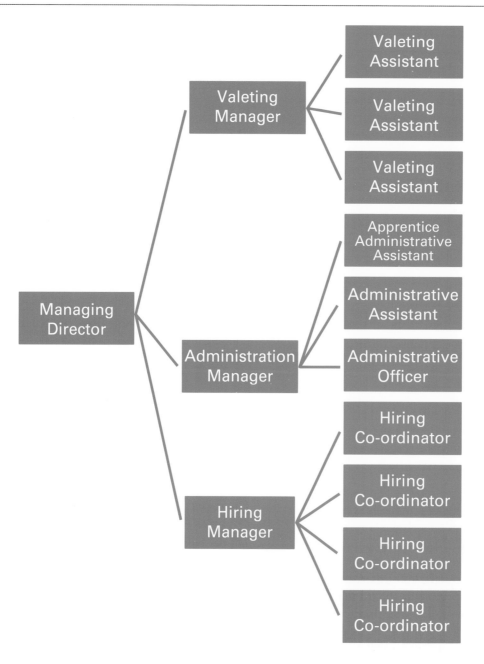

b   How many members of staff is the Hiring Manager responsible for?

Answer:

_____

c   How many members of staff report directly to the Managing Director?

Answer:

_____

d   How many members of staff, including the Managing Director, work at Ajax?

Answer:

_____

QUESTION 2

The next few questions relate to the holiday entitlements and attendance bonus scheme, provided below, as they appear in the staff handbook at Ajax.

Number of years in service	Annual holiday entitlement	❖ *Additional holiday for 100% attendance*
Less than 1 year	10 days (pro rata)	N/A
1–3 years	15 days	0.5 day
4–6 years	20 days	1 day
7–9 years	25 days	1.5 days
Over 10 years	30 days	2 days

❖ *This additional holiday bonus is only applied in the year following a 100% attendance record*

a   How have the details of the holiday entitlement been presented?

Answer:

_____

b   What is the maximum annual holiday entitlement at Ajax, without taking any available additional holiday bonus into account?

Answer:

_____

c   If a member of staff has worked at Ajax for 8 years, how many days holiday are they entitled to?

Answer:

_____

d   True or false? The holiday entitlements table provided contains 3 rows and 5 columns.

Answer:

_____

e   How much additional time off would a member of staff receive if they had a 100% attendance record in the previous year and had worked for Ajax for 11 years?

Answer:

_____

f   If a member of staff had a total holiday entitlement of 20 days and 1 day attendance bonus, how long would they have worked at Ajax?

Answer:

_____

g   What is the total holiday entitlement, including attendance bonus, for a member of staff who had 100% attendance record in their previous year and has worked at Ajax for 8 years?

Answer:

_____

QUESTION 3

The next few questions relate to the staff handbook that all new members of staff at Ajax receive upon starting their employment.

a The staff handbook is designed to do which of the following?

(1) Persuade

(2) Advise

(3) Instruct

(4) Convince

Answer:

_____

b The first page of the staff handbook contains a welcome message from the Managing Director. How would this message be most likely to be presented?

(1) In memo format

(2) In charts and graphs

(3) In paragraphs

(4) In bullet points

Answer:

_____

c The staff handbook contains information about actions to take in the case of emergencies, such as discovering a fire in the workplace. This information would be best presented in which of the following forms?

(1) Flow chart

(2) Pie chart

(3) Table

(4) Line graph

Answer:

_____

d Assuming that all new employees receive basic training on how to tackle small fires in the workplace, how would it be best to illustrate the use of firefighting equipment in the staff handbook?

(1) Using signs

(2) Using diagrams

(3) Using bar charts

(4) Using tables

Answer:

_____

e The staff handbook also includes a Sales Report of how many vehicles have been hired over the previous year. The sales achieved in each quarter are displayed in the diagram below. The next few questions relate to this Sales Report.

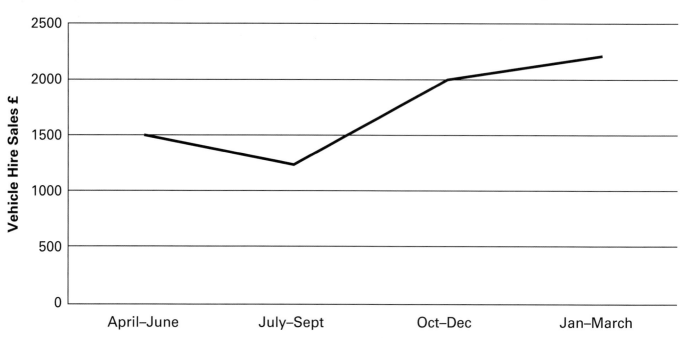

Ajax – Quarterly Vehicle Hire Sales Report

f   How has the information been presented in the Sales Report diagram?

Answer:

_____

g   In the Sales Report, during which quarter did Ajax have its highest sales?

Answer:

_____

h   According to the Sales Report, in which quarter did Ajax have its biggest sales increase?

Answer:

_____

QUESTION 4

The next few questions relate to a local large manufacturing business. The manufacturers have had three pupils, aged 14 and 15, who have attended for work experience, as part of an arrangement with the local High School. They have worked really well over the last three months and have fitted into the team of seven administrators extremely well. As a reward and a team-bonding exercise, the Administration Manager decides to ask the Finance Manager and team to look after the Administration Department on a Wednesday afternoon and take the team out to a 'Handmade Chocolate Making Workshop'. She gains parental permission, via the High School, to include the three pupils in the outing.

This table shows the course prices for the Chocolate Making Workshop.

	1 March – 21 March 29 Sept – 13 Nov £	22 March – 12 July 21 Aug – 28 Sept £	13 July – 20 Aug £
Adult	15	21	24
Child (10–15)	7	12	14

a   How much will it cost the Administration Manager to take the work experience pupils, the whole team and herself, to the workshop on 15 March?

Answer:

_____

b   The Chocolate Making Workshop also operates a retail outlet that sells handmade chocolates to the public. It opens four days a week. This table shows the days and the expected number of people to visit each day. The Workshop estimates that usually on a Wednesday, 40% of the customers buy truffle selection packs. How many truffle selection packs must they make sure to stock?

Monday	Wednesday	Friday	Saturday
150	90	225	250

Answer:

_____

c The Chocolate Making Workshop records the number of customers who visit the retail outlet on a Saturday. The chart shows the results.

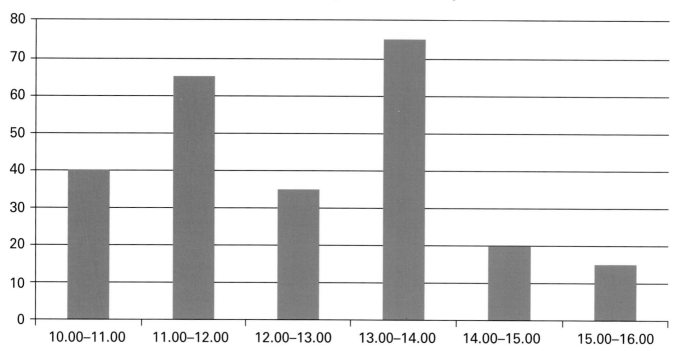

Number of customers visiting the retail outlet per hour

During which 3-hour period did the greatest number of customers visit the retail outlet?

Answer:

_____

QUESTION 5

You work in administration for Cool Print, a company that prints compliment slips.

The cost of their compliment slips is shown in the table below.

Full-colour compliment slips (210 mm × 99 mm)					
Quantity	50	500	1000	2500	5000
Price	£19.99	£49.99	£59.99	£89.99	£119.99
UK P&P	£5.00	£10.00	£10.00	£10.00	£10.00

Geoff wants to order 2500 of these compliment slips.

a How much will the slips cost (not including postage)?

_____

b How much is the postage?

_____

c What will be the total cost of the compliment slips?

_____

d What would be the total cost of ordering 50 of these compliment slips?

_____

Short-answer questions

Specific instructions to students

- The following questions will help you improve your understanding of calculations of volume, area, capacity and circumference.
- Read the following questions, then answer accordingly.

QUESTION 1

We always buy the birthday cakes for office staff from "Supacake". Their cakes are always 20 cm in diameter. What is the shortest length of ribbon that would fit round the outside of the cake?

Answer:

_____

QUESTION 2

A semi-circular window in the staff canteen has a diameter of 1.6 m. The window frame is made of plastic strips along the outside edge. What is the total length of the plastic strip around the window?

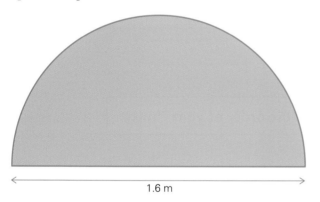

1.6 m

Answer:

_____

QUESTION 3

The diagram below (not to scale) shows the work surface of an office desk:

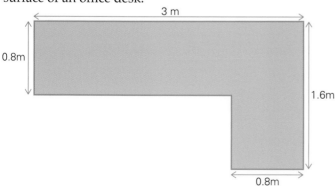

What is the area of the work surface?

Answer:

_____

QUESTION 4

A sheet of card measures 20 cm by 30 cm. What is the maximum number of circular names badges, of diameter 60 mm, that can be cut from this piece of card for visitors to the business?

Answer:

_____

QUESTION 5

A cube has sides of length 8 cm. What is the volume of the cube?

Answer:

_____

QUESTION 6

A waste bin in the office is in the shape of a cylinder. The diameter of the base is 20 cm and the height is 25 cm. What is the volume of the waste bin?

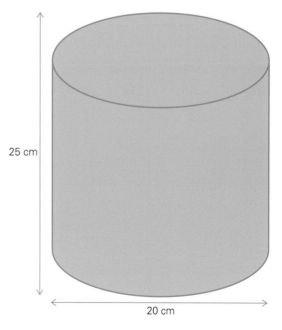

25 cm

20 cm

Answer:

_____

Unit 18:
Practice Written Exam for Business Administration

Section A: English

Section B: Mathematics

QUESTION and ANSWER BOOK

Section	Topic	Number of questions	Marks
A	English	24	154
B	Mathematics	13	118
		Total 37	Total 272

The sections may be completed in the order of your choice.

Speaking, Listening and Communication
Task 1: Informal Discussion

12 marks

You are organizing a party to celebrate raising £1 million. This event will be advertised as the 'One Million Pound Party'. Your manager has asked you and your friends to plan three money-raising activities.

Chairperson	**Alex**
Your role is to lead and control the meeting. You must manage time, encourage discussion, deal with any disagreements and write down any plans and arrangements. You need to set tasks for members in the group.	Your role is to carry out research into raffle activities. You need to share and discuss your ideas with others in the group.
Sam	**Ali**
Your role is to carry out research into quiz activities. You need to share and discuss your ideas with others in the group	Your role is to carry out research into karaoke activities. You need to share and discuss your ideas with others in the group.

Task 2: Formal meeting

15 marks

You have shared ideas for fund-raising activities to take place at the 'One Million Party'. You now have a formal meeting with your manager to discuss the ideas, planning and support you will need.

You will be marked on:

- preparation for the discussion

- making relevant and detailed contributions to the discussion

- responding appropriately to other people

- presenting information and your own point of view clearly to others

- making different types of contributions to the discussion

- using appropriate language.

Task 3: A Discussion (15 minutes)

12 marks

You are organizing a party to celebrate raising £1 million. This event will be advertised as the 'One Million Pound Party'. One of the senior managers at the charity has asked you and some colleagues to plan money-raising activities for all ticket holders on the night. He/she feels this will make the event more exciting.

Chairperson
Your role is to lead and control the meeting. You must manage time, encourage discussion, deal with any disagreements and write down any plans and arrangements. You need to set tasks for members in the group.

Alex
Your role is to carry out research in to raffle activities. You need to share and discuss your ideas with others in the group.

Sam
Your role is to carry out research into quiz activities. You need to share and discuss your ideas with others in the group

Ali
Your role is to carry out research into karaoke activities. You need to share and discuss your ideas with others in the group.

Les
Your role is to carry out research into general fundraising ideas /activities. You need to share and discuss your ideas with others in the group

Task 4: Speaking and listening (15 minutes)

15 marks

Senior managers need to be informed about the plans for the celebration. You need to present the information persuasively to one senior manager (this could be the tutor in role).

Learners need to consider what support they will use:

Microsoft Office PowerPoint	**Cue-cards**	**Images**
Physical resources	**Research summary**	**Presentation plan (introduction, middle, end)**
Projector	**Interactive whiteboard**	**Flip chart**

You will be marked on:

- preparation for the discussion

- making relevant and detailed contributions to the discussion

- responding appropriately to other people

- presenting information and your own point of view clearly to others

- making different types of contributions to the discussion

- using appropriate language

- presenting relevant information and ideas clearly

- presenting where appropriately, persuasively to others

- adapting your presentation to suit the audience, purpose and situation

- using visual aids, if appropriate, to make an effective presentation.

Reading

Organizing a Party

You and your manager (Mr Mahmood) are organizing a party for your store's 50th birthday. Your manager would like you to consider using last year's Christmas party venue. He gives you a promotion article from a magazine about a party venue (Document 1) and a letter from a previous party planner (Document 2).

You have **45 minutes** to read the documents and answer the questions below. You should spend about **5–10 minutes** of this time reading the documents.

Document 1:

Promotional Article

Eastside Hotel Review

By Jane Summer

This is an attractive and pleasant venue for a party. What a fabulous experience I had last Saturday at Eastside, where I held my own birthday party! It has a warm, friendly and welcoming atmosphere with outstanding hospitality.

IT'S DIFFERENT!
I feel there is something quite special about Eastside. It is really very different. It's fresh and unstuffy. It is so very modern, and oozes glamour and style. It makes you feel like a celebrity!

FOOD AND DRINKS
The food was excellent and they offer free drinks to all party guests for the first hour.

OVERNIGHT STAY
I really indulged myself and stayed over after the party in a luxurious room that was really quite inexpensive. The accommodation is really good value for money.

LOCATION
Eastside is set in 10 acres of beautiful landscaped gardens and is the nearest hotel to Parker's House, recently voted Britain's finest stately home. Guests even get a free pass for Parker's House as a special incentive!

My verdict: 10/10

To find out more visit their webpage:
www.eastside.com
or telephone: 0546 3456540

Document 2:

Su Win
22 Market Street
Burlington
B11 9HL
June 4th 2013

Mr R Mahmood
Bent's Retail Outlet
29 Newton Road
London
LW2 3KL

Dear Mr Mahmood

I am pleased to hear that your organization's 50th birthday party will take place this year. I feel it is important that we hold the party because it will make staff feel appreciated. Additionally, it will encourage staff to continue to work successfully within your retail outlet. However, I have been told that the Eastside Hotel is being considered as a possible venue for the event.

As you are aware, I organized a Christmas party at Eastside on behalf of Bent's Retail Outlet. This event turned out to be very expensive and the staff were rather unhelpful and unfriendly. Unfortunately, the choice of food was poor, as there were only two options for each course. There were 100 people at the party and only five members of staff so service was very slow and the food was cold.

On a brighter note, their disco was absolutely excellent. The DJ was very entertaining and played pop music all night. The dance floor was always full. He also had some really good games to break things up a bit.

There is limited accommodation at Eastside and people were disappointed that they could not stay over as it was fully booked.

I think that most people would prefer the party not to take place at Eastside.

Yours sincerely
Su Win

Answer all the questions using information from the documents. You do not need to write in sentences.

QUESTION 1   2 marks

Give two reasons why Su Win feels it is important to hold a party.

Answer:

_____

_____

QUESTION 2   1 mark

According to Document 2, what type of music did the DJ play at the party last year?

(1) House music

(2) Dance music

(3) Pop music

(4) Reggae music

Answer:

_____

QUESTION 3   4 marks

Give four reasons why Su Win does not recommend Eastside.

Answer:

_____

_____

_____

_____

QUESTION 4   5 marks

Name five things Jane Summer likes about Eastside.

Answer:

_____

_____

_____

_____

_____

_____

_____

QUESTION 5   2 marks

What could you do if you needed to find out anything else about Eastside?

Answer:

_____

_____

QUESTION 6   4 marks

a   Do you think Eastside would be a good venue for the party?

Answer:

_____

b   Explain the reasons for your choice

Answer:

_____

QUESTION 7   2 marks

Using a dictionary – explain the word *oozes*.

Answer:

_____

_____

_____

QUESTION 8   2 marks

Using a dictionary – explain the word *indulge*.

Answer:

_____

_____

_____

QUESTION 9   3 marks

In Document 1, how does Jane Summer encourage you to book a party at Eastside?

Answer:

_____

_____

_____

_____

_____

Organizing a Party

You and some colleagues are organizing the 'One Million Pound Party'. The senior managers like your ideas but have asked you to consider two venues. They give you a local magazine article / promotional piece about a party venue (Document 1), a letter from a previous party organizer (Document 2) and emails from employees (Document 3).

You have **45 minutes** to read the documents and answer the questions below. You should spend about **5–10 minutes** of this time reading the documents.

Document 1

Promotional Article

Eastside Hotel Review

By Jane Summer

This is an attractive and pleasant venue for a party. What a fabulous experience I had last Saturday at Eastside, where I held my own birthday party! It has a warm, friendly and welcoming atmosphere with outstanding hospitality.

IT'S DIFFERENT!

I feel there is something quite special about Eastside. It is really very different. It's fresh and unstuffy. It is so very modern, and oozes glamour and style. It makes you feel like a celebrity!

FOOD AND DRINKS

The food was excellent and they offer free drinks to all party guests for the first hour.

OVERNIGHT STAY

I really indulged myself and stayed over after the party in a luxurious room that was really quite inexpensive. The accommodation is really good value for money.

LOCATION

Eastside is set in 10 acres of beautiful landscaped gardens and is the nearest hotel to Parker's House, recently voted Britain's finest stately home. Guests even get a free pass for Parker's House as a special incentive!

My verdict: 10/10

Document 2:

Mr R Stapleton
Charity Ten Office House
37 Gable Rise
London
SW7 4NW

Dear Mr Stapleton

RE: Fund raising party event 2013

As you are aware, I organized the above event on behalf of Charity Ten in January of this year. I feel it would be most helpful if I provided you with feedback to help you in planning future events.

The party took place at Bongos. This was relatively cheap and the staff were extremely friendly. It is a very traditional place with traditional English food. Unfortunately, the choice of food was poor, as there were only two options for each course. There were 100 people at the party and only 5 members of staff, so service was very slow and the food was cold. They do offer a buffet party package which would have improved the event tremendously.

Their disco was absolutely excellent. The DJ was very entertaining and played popular music all night. The dance floor was always full. He also had some really good games to break things up a bit.

Unfortunately, Bongos does not have any accommodation and people were disappointed that they could not stay over.

My colleague, Paula, has mentioned that Eastside is being considered for the Million Pound Party. She has been to an event there recently with her husband and says it has a very modern day feel about it, with light and airy spaces. She does not want to feel old and says that Eastside makes you feel young and lively.

Another colleague mentioned that he thought it would be a good idea to go to Eastside, as the food is very good. He also suggested that a fancy dress theme would be good as this would make it much more fun, with a prize for the best costume.

I think most people would like the party to take place at Eastside.

Yours sincerely,

Rajesh Kapoor

Deputy Fundraising Manager

Document 3:

To: r.stapleton@charityten.co.uk

From: j.key@charityten.co.uk

Subject: Million Pound Party

Roger,

I have recently heard that Eastside may be booked for the million pound party. I would like to comment that when we went to the party at Bongos my colleagues and I had an excellent night. We had a good choice of food and the service was really fast. Their DJ is very good, with fabulous music and he even arranged for us to do some karaoke. I would very much plead with you to book Bongos again this time; otherwise I am afraid I do not think I would want to go to the million pound party.

Thanks,

Jon

To: r.stapleton@charityten.co.uk

From: m.lax@charityten.co.uk

Subject: Million Pound Party

Roger,

I have heard that Eastside is being considered as a possible venue for the forthcoming party. I went there last year and my friends and I thought the venue was not ideal. The food was very 'new cuisine' with ungenerous servings. The service was poor, the venue was unpleasant and the drinks were very expensive. The venue generally was too fashionable in my eyes, with too many modern paintings on the walls. We need a party at a venue with a more traditional feel and if the party is to be held at Eastside then I will not be purchasing a ticket. I beg you to consider this viewpoint.

Cheers,

Max

To: r.stapleton@charityten.co.uk

From: j.ronksley@charityten.co.uk

Subject: Million Pound Party

Roger,

Les has mentioned that the million pound party may be arranged at Eastside. This would be not be a good venue. I was disappointed when we last went there because the car park is so far from the party room. People do not like to walk a long distance from the car. This really spoilt the night for me and my family. Can you please make sure we book Bongos for the million pound party as they have car parking directly outside the party room?

Many thanks,

Julie

Answer all the questions using information from the documents. You do not need to write in sentences.

QUESTION 1   3 marks

What is the purpose of each document?

Answer:

_____

_____

_____

_____

_____

_____

_____

QUESTION 2   3 marks

Explain what is meant by the term 'contemporary' as used by Jane Summer. Identify three examples of a 'contemporary' feature of Eastside given in the documents.

Answer:

_____

_____

_____

QUESTION 3   4 marks

Compare and contrast the views of Jane Summer and Rajesh Kapoor's colleague, Paula, on the importance of being in a contemporary place at a party. Explain to what extent they agree or differ.

Answer:

_____

_____

_____

_____

_____

_____

_____

_____

_____

_____

_____

_____

_____

QUESTION 4   4 marks

Compare and contrast Su Win's views about Bongos with the experiences of Jon.

Answer:

_____

_____

_____

_____

_____

_____

_____

_____

_____

_____

_____

_____

_____

QUESTION 5   3 marks

In your opinion, which is the most suitable venue for the million pound party? Provide reasons for your choice.

Answer:

_____

_____

_____

_____

_____

_____

_____

QUESTION 6   3 marks

Describe the techniques used by the writers to persuade the reader in Document 1 and Document 3.

Answer:

_____

_____

_____

_____

_____

_____

_____

_____

_____

_____

_____

QUESTION 7   5 marks

Which of the three documents do you think contains the most evidence of bias? Give evidence to support your answer and explain why being aware of bias is important when organizing the outing. You may focus on one document, or on more than one.

Answer:

_____

_____

_____

_____

_____

_____

_____

_____

_____

_____

_____

_____

_____

_____

_____

_____

_____

_____

Writing

- There are two tasks which assess your writing skills.

- For both tasks, remember to write in sentences, using accurate spelling, punctuation and grammar. Allow time to check your work.

- Remember that spelling, punctuation and grammar will be assessed in both tasks.

BARNTON WATER PARK

Open 7 days a week

We need a number of
full-time and part-time staff
to work in our busy gift shops.

Must be enthusiastic and able to work as part of a team.

Interested? Please send a letter of application to the manager:
David Brownley, Barnton Water Park,
Runcorn Lane, High Legh WA11 5LB

Please state your availability for work. Give details of skills and any previous experience.

QUESTION 1   15 marks

You find this job advert in your local newspaper and decide to apply.

Write a letter of application to the manager of Barnton Water Park.

In your letter you should include:

- Where you saw the job advertised

- Details about yourself and your skills

- Previous experience or qualifications

- Your availability for work

You should:

- Use correct letter format

- Write in full sentences

- Use correct spelling, punctuation and grammar

Plan your answer before you write your final letter.

You should spend approximately 20 minutes writing this letter.

Answer:

HIGH TOP FASHION TRAINERS

£36.99

★★★★★

<u>(23 customer reviews)</u>

<u>Write a review</u>

Colour: Black

Code: 11777777

Product information

Black High Top Trainers.
Canvas upper with white laces
and white rubber sole and toe,
synthetic inner.

QUESTION 2   **10 marks**

A customer recently used the website above to buy a
pair of these trainers from your company.

She is complaining that the trainers have only been
worn a few times and they are falling apart.

Write an email to the customer replying to her
complaint.

You may wish to include:

• what she wants you to (replace or refund)

• more detail about the reason for the fault

• a solution to the problem.

Answer:

From: customerservices@shoeworld.co.uk

To: you@youremail.co.uk

Subject: Complaint

Writing

- There are two tasks which assess your writing skills.

- For both tasks, remember to write in sentences, using accurate spelling, punctuation and grammar. Allow time to check your work.

- Remember that spelling, punctuation and grammar will be assessed in both tasks.

QUESTION 1

10 marks

You are organising a party with a few colleagues to celebrate having raised £1 million pound. This party will be called the 'one million pound party'. You want to write an email to all the staff at Charity Ten to tell them what you are planning. You have organised a venue, some activities, food and drinks. You need to persuade the staff to attend the party and say why it will be successful. The email address is allstaff@charityten.co.uk

Set your email out here:

Answer:

QUESTION 2

You and some colleagues are organising the 'One Million Pound Party'. The senior manager likes your ideas but has asked you to consider two venues. He has given you a local magazine article/promotional piece about a party venue (Document 1), a letter from a previous party organiser (Document 2) and emails from employees (Document 3). Read the following documents, then write a formal letter back to the senior manager to tell him about your choice of venue and reasons why, using an appropriate format. Plan your answer before you write your draft and final letter. The Senior Manager's address is:

Mr R Stapleton

Charity Ten Office House

37 Gable Rise

London

SW7 4NW

Document 1:

Promotional Article
Eastside Hotel Review
By Jane Summer

This is an attractive and pleasant venue for a party. What a fabulous experience I had last Saturday at Eastside, where I held my own birthday party! It has a warm, friendly and welcoming atmosphere with outstanding hospitality.

IT'S DIFFERENT!
I feel there is something quite special about Eastside. It is really very different. It's fresh and unstuffy. It is so very modern, and oozes glamour and style. It makes you feel like a celebrity!

FOOD AND DRINKS
The food was excellent and they offer free drinks to all party guests for the first hour.

OVERNIGHT STAY
I really indulged myself and stayed over after the party in a luxurious room that was really quite inexpensive. The accommodation is really good value for money.

LOCATION
Eastside set in 10 acres of beautiful landscaped gardens and is the nearest hotel to Parker's House, recently voted Britain's finest stately home. Guests even get a free pass for Parker's House as a special incentive!

My verdict: 10/10

Document 2:

Mr R Stapleton
Charity Ten Office House
37 Gable Rise
London
SW7 4NW

Dear Mr Stapleton

RE: Fund raising party event 2013

As you are aware, I organized the above event on behalf of Charity Ten in January of this year. I feel it would be most helpful if I provided you with feedback to help you in planning future events.

The party took place at Bongos. This was relatively cheap and the staff were extremely friendly. It is a very traditional place with traditional English food. Unfortunately, the choice of food was poor, as there were only two options for each course. There were 100 people at the party and only 5 members of staff, so service was very slow and the food was cold. They do offer a buffet party package which would have improved the event tremendously.

Their disco was absolutely excellent. The DJ was very entertaining and played popular music all night. The dance floor was always full. He also had some really good games to break things up a bit.

Unfortunately, Bongos does not have any accommodation and people were disappointed that they could not stay over.

My colleague, Paula, has mentioned that Eastside is being considered for the Million Pound Party. She has been to an event there recently with her husband and says it has a very modern day feel about it, with light and airy spaces. She does not want to feel old and says that Eastside makes you feel young and lively.

Another colleague mentioned that he thought it would be a good idea to go to Eastside, as the food is very good. He also suggested that a fancy dress theme would be good as this would make it much more fun, with a prize for the best costume.

I think most people would like the party to take place at Eastside.

Yours sincerely,

Rajesh Kapoor

Deputy Fundraising Manager

Document 3:

To: r.stapleton@charityten.co.uk

From: j.key@charityten.co.uk

Subject: Million Pound Party

Roger,

I have recently heard that Eastside may be booked for the million pound party. I would like to comment that when we went to the party at Bongos my colleagues and I had an excellent night. We had a good choice of food and the service was really fast. Their DJ is very good, with fabulous music and he even arranged for us to do some karaoke. I would very much plead with you to book Bongos again this time; otherwise I am afraid I do not think I would want to go to the million pound party.

Thanks,

Jon

To: r.stapleton@charityten.co.uk

From: m.lax@charityten.co.uk

Subject: Million Pound Party

Roger,

I have heard that Eastside is being considered as a possible venue for the forthcoming party. I went there last year and my friends and I thought the venue was not ideal. The food was very 'new cuisine' with ungenerous servings. The service was poor, the venue was unpleasant and the drinks were very expensive. The venue generally was too fashionable in my eyes, with too many modern paintings on the walls. We need a party at a venue with a more traditional feel and if the party is to be held at Eastside then I will not be purchasing a ticket. I beg you to consider this viewpoint.

Cheers,

Max

To: r.stapleton@charityten.co.uk

From: j.ronksley@charityten.co.uk

Subject: Million Pound Party

Roger,

Les has mentioned that the million pound party may be arranged at Eastside. This would be not be a good venue. I was disappointed when we last went there because the car park is so far from the party room. People do not like to walk a long distance from the car. This really spoilt the night for me and my family. Can you please make sure we book Bongos for the million pound party as they have car parking directly outside the party room?

Many thanks,

Julie

Set your letter here:

Answer:

Section B: General Mathematics

- You should give details of your method of solution where appropriate
- Unless stated, diagrams are not drawn to scale.
- Scale drawing solutions will not be acceptable where you are asked to calculate.

Test 1

QUESTION 1   6 marks

Amir, Bethany, Clive and Davina were the finalists in a quiz competition. In the final there were five rounds with ten questions for each competitor in each round. They gained one point for each correct answer.

After **three** rounds the positions and scores were as follows.

Position	Name	Score
1	Bethany	24
2	Davina	23
3	Amir	20
4	Clive	19

In **Round 4**, Amir answered 8 questions correctly, Bethany answered 5 questions correctly, Clive answered 8 questions correctly and Davina answered 9 questions correctly.

In **Round 5**, Amir answered all 10 questions correctly and the other three each answered 7 of their questions correctly.

Complete the final table after all **five** rounds showing the position and score for each competitor.

Position	Name	Score
1		
2		
3		
4		

Who would have been the winner if the points gained in the last round (Round 5) were doubled?

Answer:

_____

QUESTION 2   15 marks

Your youth club arranges an entertainment evening at the community hall.

You have been asked to present a report on how much money was spent (Costs), how much money was collected (Income) and the profit made on the event.

You have the following information.

- The hall was hired for 4 hours at a cost of £25 per hour.

- 200 tickets were printed at a cost using the formula **Cost = Fixed cost of £10 + £5 for every 50 tickets**.

- Cost of food for making refreshments was £120.

- The band's fee was £250.

- 160 tickets were sold at £3 each.

- On average, the 160 people who attended the event spent £2.50 each on refreshments.

Remember to present your report clearly.

Answer:

QUESTION 3   9 marks

The diagram below is a scale drawing showing the positions of 4 points *A*, *B*, *P* and *Q* on level ground.

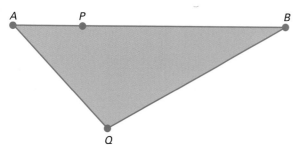

Scale: 1 cm represents 1 km

There are 2 possible routes to walk from *A* to *B*. You can walk from *A* to *P* to *B*, or you can walk from *A* to *Q* to *B*.

The different walking conditions between the points means that your average speed would be 4 km per hour between *A* and *P*, 6 km per hour between *P* and *B*, and 5 km per hour along the whole route from *A* through *Q* to *B*.

Using the scale drawing, calculate which of the two routes would be the quicker and by how much.

Answer:

QUESTION 4   11 marks

A supermarket sells a brand of tinned salmon in tins of two sizes.

It states on all tins that for health reasons the salmon must be eaten within two days of the tin being opened.

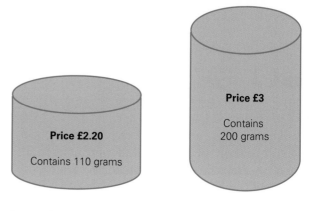

What is the price charged per 10 grams of salmon for each tin?

Answer:

Why would someone buy two small tins rather than one big tin?

Answer:

Bags containing 10 tangerines are sold at the supermarket for £1.20. A special offer advertises

Buy 2 bags for £2

Alex buys just one bag. Liam buys two bags on the special offer.

During the following week Alex ate all of her tangerines, but Liam only ate 16 of his tangerines, as the other four had gone bad.

By calculating the price of a single tangerine eaten by Alex and the price of a single tangerine eaten by Liam, who do you think had the better deal?

Answer:

The table below gives 3 measurements, both in gallons and litres.

Gallons	4	15	20
Litres	18	68	91

On the graph paper below, use the data in the table to draw a conversion graph between gallons and litres.

Use your graph to find an estimate for:

7 gallons in litres

Answer:

50 litres in gallons

Answer:

450 litres in gallons

Answer:

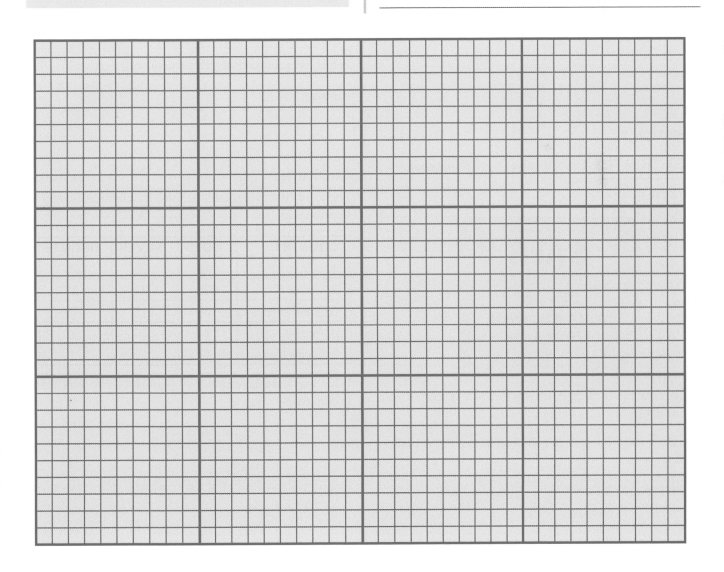

QUESTION 6   7 marks

In a hockey league, teams are awarded 3 points for a win, 1 point for a draw and 0 points if they lose a match.

A team called Burnhill Sticks is top of the league and has won 12 games, drawn 4 and lost 2. How many points does the team have?

Answer:

_____

Four other teams in the league have 29 points each.

These teams have each won a **different** number of matches.

Complete the table below to show **four** possible ways of gaining 29 points after playing 18 games.

Played	Won	Drawn	Lost	Points
18				29
18				29
18				29
18				29

For working:

QUESTION 7   5 marks

A shop on the High Street displays the following sign:

You have £22.

SALE

20% OFF
When you spend
£25 or more

How many boxes of chocolates priced at £5 each can you afford to buy?

You must show all your calculations in order to explain your answer.

Answer:

Test 2

QUESTION 1   6 marks

Eight competitors run in a race at an athletics meeting.

The name and the time for each competitor are shown in the table below.

Complete the POSITION column to show the position of each competitor.

NAME	TIME	POSITION
Khan	2 min 10 sec	
Allen	1 min 42 sec	1st
Cooper	2 min 00 sec	
Peters	1 min 47 sec	2nd
Wong	1 min 55 sec	5th
Durman	2 min 04 sec	7th
Hooton	1 min 50 sec	
Selby	1 min 54 sec	

In how many seconds under two minutes did Allen complete the race?

Answer:

_____

Which two competitors finished closest together?

Answer:

_____

QUESTION 2   6 marks

The top of the medal table at the 2012 Olympic Games in London was

COUNTRY	GOLD	SILVER	BRONZE
1. U.S.A.	46	29	29
2. China	38	27	23
3. Great Britain	29	17	19
4. Russia	24	26	32
5. South Korea	13	8	7

What was the total number of medals won by the Great Britain team?

Answer:

Find the total number of gold medals won by these five countries.

Answer:

If 3 points were awarded for a gold, 2 points for a silver and 1 point for a bronze, by how many points would Russia be ahead of Great Britain?

Answer:

QUESTION 3   6 marks

Harry decides to visit his friend who lives 24 miles away. He is unsure about whether to call a taxi, use the local bus service or cycle to his friend's house.

His friend will give him a lift back home so he does not have to worry about the return journey.

TAXI
£2.50 + £1.25 per mile

Journey time
½ hour

BUS (every hour)
Fare £5.36

Journey time
55 minutes

CYCLE

Average Speed
12 miles per hour

Compare the costs and the times taken for the three methods of travel, showing all your calculations.

Which method of travel would you recommend Harry to choose?

Give one advantage and one disadvantage of your recommendation.

Answer:

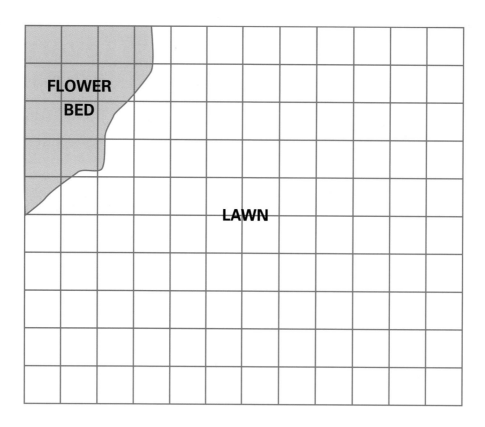

FLOWER BED

LAWN

QUESTION 4   13 marks

The garden of a house is a rectangle 12 metres long and 10 metres wide.

Calculate the area of this garden, clearly stating the units used.

Answer:

The scale diagram above, drawn on a centimetre square grid, shows the garden with a flower bed in one corner. The rest of the garden is a lawn.

Estimate the area of the lawn.

Answer:

The garden is to be fenced along the two long sides and along one of the short sides.

Posts are to be placed at 2 m intervals along these three sides.

Corner and end posts cost £3.50 each and the other posts cost £2 each.

What will be the total cost for all the posts required?

Answer:

QUESTION 5　　　　　　　　　　6 marks

The plan of a bedroom is shown on the grid below.

Scale: 1 square represents 50 cm².

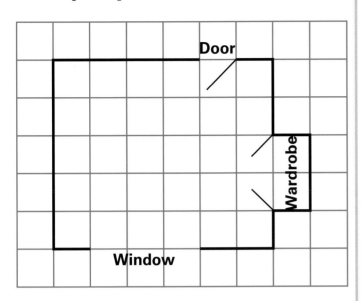

You need to position a bed and a dressing table in the bedroom.

The bed is 2 metres long and 1 metre wide.

The dressing table is 150 cm long and 50 cm wide.

Using the scale given, show where you think is the best place to position the bed and the dressing table.

QUESTION 6　　　　　　　　　　16 marks

Angela Rain's time-sheet at her work place for the week beginning 16 March 2009 is shown below.

Some of the entries are not shown.

Fill in these spaces with the correct numbers.

Angela is paid £7.50 per hour between Monday and Friday.

On a Saturday she is paid £12 per hour for working up to 1 p.m.

Calculate Angela's wage for the week shown.

Answer:

Any work done after 1 p.m. on a Saturday earns double the Saturday morning hourly rate.

Can she make up her wage to at least £400 by working on Saturday afternoon, bearing in mind that she has to leave her work place by 3.30 p.m.?

Show all of your working.

Answer:

NAME: Angela Rain			WEEK BEGINNING: 18-03-2013		
	Start	End	Hours	Lunch	Hours Worked
Monday	08.00	17.30	9½	1	8½
Tuesday	08.00	17.00		1	
Wednesday	08.30		8	½	
Thursday		17.00	9	½	8½
Friday	07.30	16.30	9		7½
Saturday	08.00	13.00	5	0	5

For working:

Business Administration Glossary

Accountant   Qualified professional who is skilled at financial reporting and business analysis.

Accounts payable   Record of funds you owe to suppliers and other business creditors for purchases of stock and overheads and other liabilities, including taxes.

Accounts receivable   Record of funds your customers owe you.

Administrative assistant   An office employee responsible for managing the office, running errands and assisting the mangers, typing, filing and other office-related duties as required by the specific job.

Annual holiday entitlement   An employee's entitlement to paid annual leave.

Appointment   An arrangement to meet someone at a particular time and place.

Appointment book   A book containing a calendar and space to keep a record of appointments.

Application form   A form that you complete in order to apply for a job.

Appointment   An arrangement to meet someone at an office or business at a particular time.

Apprenticeship   A framework consisting of an NVQ, functional skills qualification and a technical certificate. Learning takes place both in the workplace and with a learning provider.

Bank Manager   Manager of a branch of a bank.

Boardroom   A room in which the members of a board meet regularly.

Budget   An estimate of income and expenditure for a set period of time.

Business card   A small card printed with a person's name, professional occupation, business address and telephone number.

Committee   A group of people who have been assembled, especially for a specific purpose.

Computer   A machine that stores programs and information in electronic form and can be used for a variety of processes, for example, writing, calculating and communicating on the internet.

Computer visual display unit (VDU) filter   A monitor using a screen to prevent glare.

Conference   A large gathering of individuals or members of one or several organizations to discuss matters of common interest.

Cordless mouse   A mouse with no cord that transmits infrared or radio signals (RF) to a base station receiver.

Courier   A messenger who transports goods or documents in particular.

Covering letter   A letter sent with your Curriculum Vitae or Application Form to provide additional information on your skills and experience.

Credits   When cash is paid out it is recorded on the payment for credit (right hand side) of the cashbook.

Curriculum Vitae   A written description of your work experience, educational background and skills.

Customer   A person or organization that buys goods or services from a shop or other business.

Debits   When cash is received it is entered on the receipt or debit side (i.e. left hand side) of the cashbook.

Delivery notes   A document recording the delivery of products to a customer.

Discount   A deduction from the usual cost of something.

Email   A system for sending and receiving messages electronically over a computer network.

Email address   This identifies an email mailbox to which emails may be delivered.

Ergonomic keyboard   A computer keyboard designed to relieve stress on the hands and wrists, to prevent injuries.

Expenditure   Payment of cash or cash-equivalent for goods or services in settlement of a bill such as an invoice or receipt.

Flow chart   A graphic representation of a process such as a manufacturing operation, indicating the various steps taken as the product moves along the production line.

Footrest   A support on which to rest the feet.

Formal letter   A business letter written in formal language, usually when writing from one business organization to another.

Graph   A graph is an image that represents data symbolically and is used to present complex information and numerical data in a simple, compact format.

Gross earn   For individuals the total income earned in a year, as calculated prior to any tax deductions or adjustments.

Human Resources Manager   A person within an organization who is responsible for hiring new employees, training, interviewing and overseeing the Human Resources department.

Incoming mail   The arrival of mail at a certain place delivered by the Royal Mail.

Interview   A meeting to establish whether the interviewee is suitable for the job that is vacant in a business.

In-tray   A tray on a desk that holds papers relating to matters to be dealt with.

Invoice   A bill sent by a provider of a product or service to the purchaser.

Legal secretary   A person employed by a solicitor whose expertise includes the typing and filing of contracts, pleadings or other legal documents.

Letter   A written or printed communication addressed to a person or organization and usually sent by post.

Letter of complaint   A persuasive letter sent by a customer to an organization to express dissatisfaction with a product or service.

Liquid paper   Brand name of white correction fluid used on documents.

Managing Director   The person with the most senior position in an organization and with the responsibility of managing it all.

Medical receptionist   A person who greets patients and answers telephones.

Meeting   A formal or informal assembly of individuals called to debate certain issues and problems, and to take decisions.

Memo   A short message sent from one person to another in the same organization.

Microsoft Office   Brand name of a suite of computer programs for Windows and Mac, including Word, Excel, Powerpoint.

Minutes of a meeting   A written account of what happened in a meeting.

Mouse mat   A thin flat pad, usually made of rubber, on which a computer mouse is used.

Office assistant   A person who performs skilled clerical and data entry work whilst under supervision.

Office manager   A person who organizes and supervises all of the administrative activities that enable the smooth running of an office.

Outgoing mail   Mail leaving the business and being sent somewhere else.

Overtime   The amount of time someone works beyond normal working hours.

Payroll   The total amount of wages and salaries paid by an organization to its employees.

Petty cash   Relatively small amounts of cash kept at hand for making immediate payments for miscellaneous small expenses.

Petty cash book   All petty or small payments made through petty cash funds are recorded systematically.

Photocopier   A machine that uses a photographic process to produce an almost instant copy of something printed, written or drawn.

Pie chart   A circular chart divided into sectors; each sector showing the relative size of each value.

Presentation   The formal delivery of a document to the appropriate audience.

Printer   A machine for printing text or pictures onto paper, especially one linked to a computer.

Purchase order   A document authorizing a seller to deliver goods, with payments to be made at a later date

Purchasing officer   An individual within an organization responsible for purchasing the goods and services it requires.

Receipts   A printed document that is logged by a business every time cash is received for a good or service.

Receptionist   A person employed in an office or other organization to greet and deal with customers and visitors.

Registered mail   Mail registered by the post office when sent to assure safe delivery.

Report   A document that presents information in an organized format for a specific audience and purpose.

Samples   A small part or quantity intended to show what the whole is like.

Solicitor   A lawyer who traditionally deals with any legal matter including conducting procedures in court in the United Kingdom.

Staff handbook   A document that provides guidance about company policies and procedures for employees.

Stationery   General office supplies such as those needed for writing, typing, or printing.

Stock   The goods or merchandise kept on the premises of a business or warehouse available for sale or distribution.

Stocktake   To count the goods and materials owned by an organization or available for sale in a shop at a particular time.

Suppliers   Someone whose business is to supply a particular service or commodity to you.

Timesheet   A piece of paper for recording the number of hours worked.

Trade facility   A person or group of people that provide a physical or electronic facility in which multiple participants have the ability to trade agreements and contracts by accepting bids and offers made by other participants in the facility.

Training course   Courses on which you receive instruction to improve your work skills.

Travel agent   Someone who sells or arrange trips or tours for customers.

Wages   Money that is paid or received for work or services by the hour, day or week.

Warehouse manager   A person who oversees the efficient receipt, storage and dispatch of a wide range of goods stored in a warehouse.

Wholesalers   The sale of goods in large quantities, as for resale by a retailer.

Wrist rest   A platform used to raise the wrist above keyboard level for typing.

English Glossary

Adjective A type of word that describes NOUNS (things, people and places), for example *sharp*, *warm* or *handsome*.

Adverb A type of word that describes VERBS (things happening), for example *slowly*, *often* or *quickly*.

Apostrophe A PUNCTUATION mark with two main functions: (1) shows where letters have been missed out when words or phrases are shortened, for example changing *cannot* to *can't*, or *I will* to *I'll*; (2) shows where a NOUN 'possesses' something, for example *Dave's bike*, *the cat's whiskers* or *St John's Wood*.

Capital letter Used to begin a SENTENCE, to begin the names of people, days, months and places, and for abbreviations such as *RSPCA* or *FBI*.

Comma A PUNCTUATION mark that has many uses, usually to separate phrases in a long SENTENCE so that it is easier to read and understand, or to separate items in a list.

Formal language The type of language used when speaking to or writing to someone you don't know, such as your bank manager (e.g. 'I am writing to request a bank statement').

Full stop A PUNCTUATION mark used at the end of SENTENCES.

Future tense The VERB forms we use to talk about things that will happen in future (e.g. 'I *will watch* television tonight').

Homophone A word that sounds the same as another word, but has a different spelling and meaning, for example *break* and *brake*.

Informal language The type of language used when you are speaking to or writing to someone you know well, such as a friend (e.g. 'Hi, how are you? Do you fancy coming to the cinema with me?').

Instructions A series or list of statements designed to show someone how to do something, for example to use some equipment or to follow some rules.

Noun A word used to refer to a thing, person or place, for example *chair*, *George* or *Sheffield*.

Paragraph A section of writing about the same subject or topic, that begins on a new line and consists of one or more SENTENCES.

Past tense The VERB forms we use to talk about things that have happened in the past (e.g. 'I *watched* television last night').

Present tense The VERB forms we use to talk about things that are happening now (e.g. 'I *am watching* television').

Pronouns Words that are used instead of NOUNS (things, people and places), for example *he, she, we, it, who, something, ourselves*.

Punctuation Marks used in writing to help make it clear and organized, by separating or joining together words or phrases, or by adding or changing emphasis.

Question mark A PUNCTUATION mark used at the end of a question, to show that you have asked something.

Sentence A group of words, beginning with a CAPITAL LETTER and ending with a FULL STOP, QUESTION MARK or exclamation mark, put together using correct grammar, to make a meaningful statement or question, etc.

Verb Word used to indicate an action, for example *mix*, *smile* or *walk*.

Mathematics Glossary

Actual   The exact calculation of a set of numbers.

Analogue clock   A clock that displays minute and hour hands and shows the time changing continuously.

Area   The size of a surface; the amount of space in a two-dimensional shape or property, e.g. the floor space of a room or flat.

Decimal   A way of organizing numbers based around the number ten (the most familiar system used in the world today).

Decimal point   A mark, often a full stop, used in a number to divide between whole numbers and FRACTIONS of whole numbers shown in DECIMAL form.

Digital clock   A clock that tells the time using numbers instead of hands and shows the time changing digitally – from one exact value to the next.

Estimate   (1) A calculation that requires a rough guess rather than working out the actual figure; (2) to work out this value.

Fraction   A quantity or amount that is not a whole number, e.g. less than 1. A part of a whole number.

Imperial   The British system of units for weights and measures before the METRIC system, including pounds, stones, miles, feet and inches.

Mean   A form of average of a set of numbers. To calculate the mean, add all of the numbers together and then divide by how many numbers there are.

Median   A form of average of a set of numbers. To calculate the median, place the numbers in numerical order and then find the middle number.

Metric   An international DECIMAL system of units for weights and measures, including kilograms, grams, kilometres, metres and centimetres.

Mode   A form of average of a set of numbers. To calculate the mode, look for the number that appears most often.

Percentage   A proportion, or FRACTION, that means part of one hundred.

Perimeter   The total lengths of all of the sides of a two-dimensional shape or AREA, e.g. the distance around the outside of a room.

Range   The difference between the largest and smallest numbers in a set of figures.

Ratio   A way to compare the amounts of things – how much of one thing there is compared to how much of another thing.

Scales   An instrument used to measure the weight of an object or person.

Volume   The amount of three-dimensional space that an object occupies.

Formulae and Data

Circumference of a Circle

$C = \pi \times d$
where: C = circumference, π = 3.14, d = diameter

Diameter of a Circle

$d = \frac{C}{\pi}$
Where: C = circumference, π = 3.14, d = diameter

Area

$A = l \times b$

Area = length × breadth and is given in square units

Volume of a Cube

$V = l \times w \times h$

Volume = length × width × height and is given in cubic units

Volume of a Cylinder

$V_c = \pi \times r^2 \times h$

Where: V_c = volume of a cylinder, π = 3.14, r = radius, h = height

Times Tables

1

1 × 1	=	1
2 × 1	=	2
3 × 1	=	3
4 × 1	=	4
5 × 1	=	5
6 × 1	=	6
7 × 1	=	7
8 × 1	=	8
9 × 1	=	9
10 × 1	=	10
11 × 1	=	11
12 × 1	=	12

2

1 × 2	=	2
2 × 2	=	4
3 × 2	=	6
4 × 2	=	8
5 × 2	=	10
6 × 2	=	12
7 × 2	=	14
8 × 2	=	16
9 × 2	=	18
10 × 2	=	20
11 × 2	=	22
12 × 2	=	24

3

1 × 3	=	3
2 × 3	=	6
3 × 3	=	9
4 × 3	=	12
5 × 3	=	15
6 × 3	=	18
7 × 3	=	21
8 × 3	=	24
9 × 3	=	27
10 × 3	=	30
11 × 3	=	33
12 × 3	=	36

4

1 × 4	=	4
2 × 4	=	8
3 × 4	=	12
4 × 4	=	16
5 × 4	=	20
6 × 4	=	24
7 × 4	=	28
8 × 4	=	32
9 × 4	=	36
10 × 4	=	40
11 × 4	=	44
12 × 4	=	48

5

1 × 5	=	5
2 × 5	=	10
3 × 5	=	15
4 × 5	=	20
5 × 5	=	25
6 × 5	=	30
7 × 5	=	35
8 × 5	=	40
9 × 5	=	45
10 × 5	=	50
11 × 5	=	55
12 × 5	=	60

6

1 × 6	=	6
2 × 6	=	12
3 × 6	=	18
4 × 6	=	24
5 × 6	=	30
6 × 6	=	36
7 × 6	=	42
8 × 6	=	48
9 × 6	=	54
10 × 6	=	60
11 × 6	=	66
12 × 6	=	72

7

1 × 7	=	7
2 × 7	=	14
3 × 7	=	21
4 × 7	=	28
5 × 7	=	35
6 × 7	=	42
7 × 7	=	49
8 × 7	=	56
9 × 7	=	63
10 × 7	=	70
11 × 7	=	77
12 × 7	=	84

8

1 × 8	=	8
2 × 8	=	16
3 × 8	=	24
4 × 8	=	32
5 × 8	=	40
6 × 8	=	48
7 × 8	=	56
8 × 8	=	64
9 × 8	=	72
10 × 8	=	80
11 × 8	=	88
12 × 8	=	96

9

1 × 9	=	9
2 × 9	=	18
3 × 9	=	27
4 × 9	=	36
5 × 9	=	45
6 × 9	=	54
7 × 9	=	63
8 × 9	=	72
9 × 9	=	81
10 × 9	=	90
11 × 9	=	99
12 × 9	=	108

10

1 × 10	=	10
2 × 10	=	20
3 × 10	=	30
4 × 10	=	40
5 × 10	=	50
6 × 10	=	60
7 × 10	=	70
8 × 10	=	80
9 × 10	=	90
10 × 10	=	100
11 × 10	=	110
12 × 10	=	120

11

1 × 11	=	11
2 × 11	=	22
3 × 11	=	33
4 × 11	=	44
5 × 11	=	55
6 × 11	=	66
7 × 11	=	77
8 × 11	=	88
9 × 11	=	99
10 × 11	=	110
11 × 11	=	121
12 × 11	=	132

12

1 × 12	=	12
2 × 12	=	24
3 × 12	=	36
4 × 12	=	48
5 × 12	=	60
6 × 12	=	72
7 × 12	=	84
8 × 12	=	96
9 × 12	=	108
10 × 12	=	120
11 × 12	=	132
12 × 12	=	144

Multiplication Grid

×	1	2	3	4	5	6	7	8	9	10	11	12
1	1	2	3	4	5	6	7	8	9	10	11	12
2	2	4	6	8	10	12	14	16	18	20	22	24
3	3	6	9	12	15	18	21	24	27	30	33	36
4	4	8	12	16	20	24	28	32	36	40	44	48
5	5	10	15	20	25	30	35	40	45	50	55	60
6	6	12	18	24	30	36	42	48	54	60	66	72
7	7	14	21	28	35	42	49	56	63	70	77	84
8	8	16	24	32	40	48	56	64	72	80	88	96
9	9	18	27	36	45	54	63	72	81	90	99	108
10	10	20	30	40	50	60	70	80	90	100	110	120
11	11	22	33	44	55	66	77	88	99	110	121	132
12	12	24	36	48	60	72	84	96	108	120	132	144

Maths and English for Business Administration
Online Answer Guide

To access the Answer Guide for Maths and English for Business Administration follow these simple steps:

1) Copy the following link into your web browser:

http://www.cengagebrain.co.uk/shop/isbn/9781408083093

2) Click on the Free Study Tools Link.

Notes

Notes

Notes

Notes

Notes

Notes